The Only
BOOK
of
WICCAN
SPELLS
YOU'LL EVER
NEED

2nd Edition

The Only
BOOK
of
WICCAN
SPELLS
YOU'LL EVER
NEED

2nd Edition

Marian Singer, Trish MacGregor, & Skye Alexander

Adams Media
New York London Toronto Sydney New Delhi

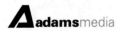

Adams Media
An Imprint of Simon & Schuster, Inc.
100 Technology Center Drive
Stoughton, MA 02072

For information about special discounts for bulk purchases, please contact Simon & Schuster Special Sales at 1-866-506-1949 or business@simonandschuster.com.

The Simon & Schuster Speakers Bureau can bring authors to your live event. For more information or to book an event contact the Simon & Schuster Speakers Bureau at 1-866-248-3049 or visit our website at www.simonspeakers.com.

Manufactured in the United States of America

12 2021

Library of Congress Cataloging-in-Publication Data has been applied for.

ISBN 978-1-4405-4275-6
ISBN 978-1-4405-4276-3 (ebook)

Contains material adapted and abridged from: *The Only Wiccan Spell Book You'll Ever Need* by Marian Singer and Trish MacGregor, copyright © 2004 by Simon & Schuster, Inc., ISBN: 978-1-59337-096-1; *Good Spells for Bad Days* by Skye Alexander, copyright © 2009 by Simon & Schuster, Inc., ISBN: 978-1-60550-131-4; *The Everything® Spells and Charms Book, 2nd Edition*, by Skye Alexander, copyright © 2008, 2001 by Simon & Schuster, Inc., ISBN: 978-1-59869-386-7; and *The Everything® Wicca and Witchcraft Book, 2nd Edition*, by Skye Alexander, copyright © 2008, 2002 by Simon & Schuster, Inc., ISBN: 978-1-59869-404-8.

Contents

Introduction

Magick is present in all of us when we are young. We simply lose sight of it as we grow into adults and get swallowed by the stresses of day-to-day living. This book is about learning to reconnect with that magick. In these pages, you'll learn to pay attention to nature—the cycles of the moon, the power of the elements. You'll also discover how to incorporate nature's tools—crystals, stones, herbs, flowers, minerals, and such—into your magickal workings.

Given that this spell book is *The Only Book of Wiccan Spells You'll Ever Need*, you might be surprised to find it's not a hefty, verbose tome, filled with ancient magickal utterings or lengthy digressions exploring every detail of Wiccan belief. Perhaps you were even anticipating a gigantic storehouse for ingredients, an endless string of spellcasting recipes, or a slew of magickal charms and incantations. And yet, this volume is rather slim.

That's because there is no easy way to explain Wicca in a nutshell. Wicca is an ancient practice, a gentle, earth-oriented religion that seeks truth and understanding, and a way of life meant to affect inner change. Yes, it's a framework for using magickal powers. It also involves worshiping ancient Pagan deities, and it recognizes the duality of the Divine as one force that incorporates male and female, both God and Goddess. It encourages respect for nature, stresses concern for the planet, and acknowledges that the life force should be reverenced in all things, as well.

Beyond exploring basic tenets such as these, however, there is no rigid dogma in Wicca. Whether you come to Wicca from a base of traditional religion or no formalized religion at all, you can easily work Wicca into your life. Following Wicca and casting spells are highly personal experiences. Just as there is no single method for practicing Wicca, there are also very few rules set in stone when it comes to spellcasting. This doesn't mean there are no rules, mind you. For one thing, spellcasting must always seek the good of all—both for yourself and for others—and it cannot cause any harm. (You'll learn more about these basic, core principles in this book.) The point is, however, that the spells included in this book are merely meant to be representative of what spellcasting entails and how it is accomplished. To get you started, you'll find more than 125 spells in this updated second edition! The beauty of this book is that you can use its guidelines as a springboard for exploring your own ways of doing things, and eventually begin to craft your own spells as your facility for spellcraft progresses and your knowledge and experience increase.

As you're using this book, realize that Wiccan spellcasting is not about magickal power in the stereotypical sense. There's no "hocus pocus" or "abracadabra" involved here, no stirring bubbling cauldrons or flying on broomsticks. The true magick of Wicca lies in developing your own inner potential and spirituality. Remember that deep inside yourself, you already have the power to tap into the energy of the universe and the natural world around you; you just need to recognize that potential and direct it. This book is intended to help you on your journey toward getting in touch with nature, in touch with the Divine, and in touch with your inner potential, because, ultimately, that is where the real value of spellcasting lies.

Part 1

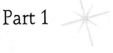

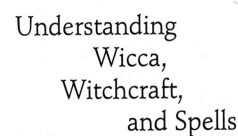

Understanding
Wicca,
Witchcraft,
and Spells

Chapter 1

The Philosophy and Ideology
of Wiccan Spellcrafting

Before you can immerse yourself in the study of spellcrafting, it's important to sort out fact from fiction when it comes to Witches and Wiccans. Unfortunately, modern culture promotes many erroneous beliefs about who Witches are and what they do. These sorts of stereotypical myths and misunderstandings need to be dispelled in order to understand the true ideals, ethics, and philosophy of Witchcraft.

Only education and understanding can uproot misconceptions and prejudices about Witchcraft and Wicca, and in reading this book, you are on the right path. It's time to start thinking of Witches and Wiccans in a new sense—as people who are simply living their lives in a uniquely magickal way. Let's begin by examining the basic ground rules and core concepts that most Witches and Wiccans hold in common.

Witches and Magick

For the purposes of simplicity, the word *Witch* will be used to describe both male and female Witches or Wiccans throughout this book. (Keep in mind that a male Witch or Wiccan is not called a Warlock. He is a Witch or Wiccan, too. *Warlock* came from an Old English word for "oath breaker," and later, during the mid-1400s, it came to mean "liar." This is a rather nasty insult!) The words *Wizard* and *Sorcerer* can also be used for a man or a woman. *Wizard* derives from a term meaning "wise," and *sorcerer* means "Witch" or "Diviner."

☀ Wiccan Wonderings: What, exactly, does Wicca mean?

Wicce, the Anglo Saxon word meaning "one who practices sorcery," is the root of the words *Witch* and *Wicca*. At first the term was applied to both wise men and women, especially those who practiced herbcraft (sometimes called "cunning arts"). After the Crusades, however, the term was used mostly for women and carried negative connotations. Nowadays, it refers to modern Witchcraft and is not considered negative.

The word *magician* is also appropriate for both sexes and for Witches as well as Wiccans. The ancient Persian prophet Zoroaster taught priests who were called Magi, and they relied heavily on astrology as an art. Depending on the cultural setting, *magician* came to describe people adept in astrology, sorcery, or other magickal arts. Note that the word *magick* in Wicca and Witchcraft is spelled with a *k*, to differentiate it from stage magic (or sleight of hand).

Which Is the Witch?

While folklore, literature, religion, and other cultural influences through the ages have often portrayed Witches in a negative light, history indicates otherwise in most cases. Despite the ugly face that these points of reference have tried to put on Witches, few, in reality, used their knowledge and abilities toward negative ends. Their heritage is that of helping and healing individuals and communities.

Most Witches learned their skills as a craft—part of a family tradition in which they were carefully trained. Villages and cities alike had honored, cunning folk to whom people would turn for all kinds of help—from encouraging crops to grow to mending a broken heart. In exchange for such services, Witches might receive a chicken, a measure of grain, or other necessities.

There was rarely any specific ethical or religious construct involved in Witchcraft unless it came from family or cultural influences, or from the individual's own sense of right and wrong. Witches do not need to believe in divine beings in order to use magick. They do not necessarily have a particular "code" or tradition to which they adhere, unless it is dictated by familial custom. This does not mean all Witches are without ethics or religion. Magick is simply a means to an end and is morally neutral (except in terms of how it's wielded).

Common Misconceptions

Perhaps the most pervasive myth is that Witches are Satanists—not true. In addition, they're more likely to wear a business suit than a pointy black hat. Most drive cars rather than ride broomsticks and prefer pizza to eye of newt any day. Here are some other common stereotypes:

- **Witches sell their souls to the devil in return for special powers: False.** This folkloric image is erroneous yet has been fostered by some mainstream religions.
- **Witches are humans who have psychic abilities: Sometimes.** This assumption may or may not be true. Some psychics may be Witches; some but not all Witches are psychic.
- **Witches are sorcerers: Yes.** This term is accurate from an anthropological point of view.
- **Witches are modern worshipers of ancient Gods and Goddesses: Sometimes.** This description is fairly accurate for Wiccans but not always for Witches.
- **Witches cast evil spells on people, either for fun or revenge, such as turning men into toads: False.** Although Witches do cast spells for people (with their permission), these spells are done to help others, not to harm them. And if they could, most Witches would rather turn frogs into princes!
- **Witches are old, ugly hags: False.** Witches come in all shapes, sizes, and ages—many are quite beautiful, and young women are eagerly joining the ranks of Wicca. This stereotype is inspired by the Crone, a woman whose child-rearing responsibilities are behind her and who can now devote herself to her Craft.

Only education and understanding can uproot misconceptions and prejudices about Witches. Many universities now offer classes in the history and practice of magick and Witchcraft. Wicca is the fastest-growing religion in America.

Where Wicca Comes In

Writers like Gerald Gardner and Sir James Frazier are commonly given credit for coining the term Wiccan and kick-starting the modern movement in the 1950s.

Although the methods and tools of the Wiccan are often the same as those of the Witch, the constructs within which Wiccans work are a little different. The primary variance is that Wicca is considered a religion, with specific rituals and moral codes similar to those of other world faiths.

Wiccan Gods and Goddesses

Many Wiccans follow a specific God or Goddess, and others honor several deities. These beings or personages may be chosen by the individual or dictated by a group, magickal tradition, or cultural standard. In this case, the Wiccan looks to the Divine as a copilot in the spiritual quest and as a helpmate in effectively and safely guiding magickal energy.

Several divine figures show up as popular favorites in the Wiccan community. Among them are:

Apollo (Greece and Rome)
Brigid (Celtic Europe)
Dagda (Ireland)
Diana (Rome)
Hecate (Greece)
Herne (Celtic Europe)
Ishtar (Middle East)

Isis (Egypt)
Pan (Greece)
Ra (Egypt)

Karmic Law

Another difference is that Wiccans and Witches view the cause and effect of their magick in different ways. Although Witches may or may not concern themselves with the potential results of a spell or ritual, Wiccans' intentions are bound by the Threefold Law, meaning that whatever they do, whether for good or harm, will come back to them three times over. This doesn't mean Witches don't respect magickal power, nor does it mean Witches are unethical. It just means that Wiccans pay particularly close attention to the laws of karma.

This short rhyme, called "The Wiccan Rede," is a guide for practitioners of Wicca and sums up the basic code of ethics Wiccans try to follow in their magickal work and in their everyday lives:

> *Bide the Wiccan law ye must*
> *In perfect love, in perfect trust,*
> *Eight words the Wiccan Rede fulfill:*
> *An' ye harm none, do what ye will.*
> *What ye send forth comes back to thee,*
> *So ever mind the Rule of Three.*
> *Follow this with mind and heart,*
> *And merry ye meet, and merry ye part.*

The Divine Feminine

Many Wiccans believe that the Divine is both feminine and masculine, so they venerate the Goddess and God. The Goddess is symbolized by Mother Earth. Concern for the environment and "green" practices demonstrate respect for the Goddess, who is manifest in all of nature. It's no accident that movements honoring the Earth and the Goddess evolved simultaneously. Indeed, many Witches believe that unless Goddess energy reawakens within each of us and in the world as a whole, the planet may be destroyed.

Witches often depict the Goddess in three stages that represent the three phases of a woman's life: maiden, mother, and crone. Celtic art illustrates this tripart nature as three interlocking pointed loops called *vesica piscis,* which symbolize the opening to the womb. Others show the feminine trinity as three phases of the moon: waxing, waning, and full.

The Maiden

The Maiden Goddess signifies youth. In this aspect, she symbolizes innocence, hope, joy, curiosity, flexibility, courage, and enthusiasm. Greco-Roman mythology expressed this phase of the Goddess as Luna, the chaste moon goddess. Diana, Artemis, Eos, Renpet, Bast, and Persephone also characterize the maiden aspect of the Divine Feminine.

In magickal work, the following can serve as symbolic associations for the Maiden:

- Baby animals (before puberty)
- The colors silver, white, and light blue
- Lightweight clothing and delicate fabrics such as gauze, lace, thin cotton, and silk
- Clear quartz, pearl, diamond, aquamarine
- The chaste tree, meadowsweet, lemongrass, white rose, hyacinth, narcissus, crocus, apple blossoms, peach blossoms, lilac, gardenia
- The morning hours of the day, from dawn until noon
- The spring months
- The waxing moon

The Mother

The Mother Goddess signifies maturity. Her attributes include fertility, creativity, nurturing, comfort, abundance, strength, sensuality, confidence, and power. Pele, Gaia, Freya, Isis, Ceres, Demeter, Brigid, Oshun, Yemaja, Aphrodite, Venus, Tara, and Mary are among the goddesses who personify the mother phase of the Divine Feminine.

In magickal work, the following can serve as symbolic associations for the Mother:

- Pregnant or nursing animals
- Rich colors: ruby red, forest green, royal blue, and amber
- Luxurious clothing and fabrics including velvet, damask, cashmere, and mohair
- Geode, emerald, turquoise, opal, coral, rose quartz, amber
- Apple, pomegranate, peach, raspberry, strawberry, red clover, red rose, mint, iris, jasmine, cinnamon, parsley, daisy, myrtle, orchid, saffron
- The afternoon hours, from noon to sunset
- Summer through the harvest season
- The full moon

The Crone

The Crone signifies the years after menopause. In some traditions, a woman is considered a Crone after she has experienced her second Saturn Return (usually at about age fifty-eight). The attributes inherent in this aspect of the Divine Feminine include wisdom, intuition, prophecy, stability, pragmatism, patience, detachment, and fortitude.

Images of Crones

The last phase of womanhood, the Crone period, is the one usually associated with stereotypical images of Witches. The traditional images of the ancient Crone or hag aren't attractive either, but that portrayal is not surprising when you consider that humans are afraid of mortality and the Crone reminds one of old age and death.

Sophia, Hecate, Ceridwen, White Buffalo Woman, Butterfly Woman, Kali, Lilith, Baba Yaga, and Kuan Yin are among the goddesses who personify the Crone phase of the Divine Feminine. In magickal work, the following can serve as symbolic associations for the Crone:

- Old animals
- Dark colors: brown, black, midnight blue, purple
- Heavy clothing (often robes) and fabrics including wool and linen
- Smoky quartz, jet, onyx, amethyst, fossils
- Holly, mandrake, pine, juniper, mistletoe, nightshade, nuts, oak, moss, wintergreen, ginseng; also dried or withered plants
- The hours from sunset to dawn
- Late fall and winter
- The waning moon

The Divine Masculine

The feminine is not complete without the masculine; together, these energetic polarities form a whole. Before the re-emergence of Goddess-centered spirituality, only the male divinity's face was present in most parts of the world. Some Wiccans and Witches concentrate on the Divine Feminine. Others, however, believe that the Divine expresses as both male and female.

Witches often depict the Divine Masculine as having three faces, which represent the stages of a man's life: youth, maturity, and old age. However, Witches aren't the only ones who envision a tripart God. Christians honor the male trinity of Father, Son, and Holy Spirit. In the Hindu religion, Brahma represents the creative principle of God, Vishnu is considered the preserver, and Shiva is the destroyer. Although the cultural aspects of these deities may differ, they still recognize the tripart expression of the masculine force.

The Son

The youthful aspect of the God is depicted as the Son. He signifies naiveté, daring, a sense of adventure, vitality, action, exuberance, and freedom. The ancient Egyptians expressed this archetype as Horus, who flies through the sky freely, with the sun in one eye and the moon in the other.

The Oak King

In magickal mythology, the Oak King represents the waxing year. This rather cocky young male takes over from the elder aspect of the God at year's end by battling him for the crown. The tale of Sir Gawain and the Green Knight is an excellent illustration of this concept, the Green Knight being the elder god.

Witches honor a Horned God, who symbolizes this youthful facet of the Divine Masculine. His wildness, sensuality, and passion make him brashly attractive. This deity expresses the Witch's connection to nature as well, and to all the primal magick therein. Cupid (the son of Venus) is another easily discernible example of the youthful virility associated with the Son.

The Father

In the Father, the mature face of God is emphasized. This aspect of the Divine Masculine represents strength, power, authority, leadership ability, protection, responsibility, and courage. He is viewed as the warrior king in some cultures, the wise ruler in others. In modern Western society, he could be seen as the capable corporate executive.

Mars, God of War

Mars, the god of war in Roman mythology, was a staunch protector of the land. He symbolizes the transition from the son aspect of the God to the father phase. Interestingly enough, another name for Mars was Marpiter (Father Mars), implying an older, more experienced deity.

Like the Goddess, the God possesses a creative aspect. Indeed, both forces are necessary for creation. The Father God in some early cultures oversaw the crafts, such as those of the "smiths," who were regarded as magick workers in their own right. Hephaestus, originally a fire god in Lycia and Asia Minor, eventually became the god of craftspeople in Greece. He earned this reputation by constructing palaces for the gods and fashioning Zeus's thunderbolts. This creative aspect of the Father can also be seen in the figure of Bahloo, the Australian aborigine All-Father, whose job was to create all animals and people with his consort.

The Grandfather

The elder aspect of the masculine deity, or Grandfather, is as wise and wily as his female consort. He oversees the underworld (the place where souls are said to go between lives), destiny, death, resurrection, and justice. Like those of the Crone's, his concerns extend beyond the physical world and involve the process of transformation, assimilation of knowledge, and movement between the various levels of existence.

The Grandfather in the Tarot Deck

In a tarot deck, the grandfather aspect of the God energy is illustrated as The Hermit. This card usually shows a bearded old man dressed in long robes, retreating into the darkness. However, he holds a lantern high, shining light to illuminate the way for those who wish to follow and learn what he knows.

The mythological elder god, known as the Holly King (who battles with the Oak King), is one version of the grandfather archetype. Truthfully, the grandfather could win this battle with his wits if he so chooses. Nonetheless, he allows himself to lose so that The Wheel of the Year (see Chapter 2) will keep turning.

Honoring and Invoking Deities

Many Witches believe that divine assistance is always available to you and that gods and goddesses gladly offer their guidance, help, and energy to humans to use for positive purposes. Some view divine beings as higher aspects of human consciousness, which can be accessed and activated through magickal means.

Ask First!

If you want to connect with a particular entity, first ask that god or goddess to listen to your request and come to your aid. One theory states that deities will not interfere with your own free will—you must ask them sincerely for help.

If you aren't used to considering a divine being as a partner in your spiritual and practical pursuits, you may wonder how to go about petitioning your favorite god or goddess for assistance. Here are a few suggestions:

- Make an offering of some sort to the deity. Burning incense is a popular offering, although you may wish to choose an offering that more specifically corresponds to the nature of the deity whose help you seek.
- Place a figurine of the chosen deity on your altar and focus your attention on it.
- Use an oracle, such as tarot cards or runes, to access divine wisdom and open your mind to messages from the deities.
- Pray.
- Meditate.
- Light a candle in honor of the deity you wish to petition.
- Design and perform a ritual to the deity.
- Write your request on a slip of paper, then burn it.
- Choose a crystal or gemstone that relates to the deity (see Chapter 4). Carry the stone in your pocket and touch it periodically.
- Plant herbs or flowers in honor of the god or goddess. Choose plants that correspond to the deity's nature and your intent, such as roses for love or mint for prosperity (see Chapter 4).

The following list of dieties may be useful as you plan your spellwork.

Deities from Around the World

Goddess	Areas of Governance
Amaterasu	Beauty, leadership
Aphrodite	Love, beauty, sensuality
Artemis	Courage, independence, protection
Bast	Playfulness, joy, freedom
Brigid	Creativity, inspiration, healing
Ceres	Nourishment, health
Ceridwin	Inspiration, wisdom
Concordia	Peace
Cybele	Fertility
Freya	Love, healing, sensuality
Hecate	Wisdom
Inanna	Journeys, facing fears, courage, grief
Kuan Yin	Compassion, forgiveness
Lakshmi	Wealth, abundance
Pele	Fiery spirit, destruction and rebirth, vitality
Sekhmet	Grace, dignity, strength
Sophia	Wisdom, power
Tiamat	Power, protection
God	Areas of Governance
Agassou	Protection, guidance
Apollo	Beauty, poetry, music
Ganesh	Strength, perseverance, overcoming obstacles
God	Areas of Governance
Green Man	Fertility, nature, abundance, sexuality

Deities from Around the World

Horus	Knowledge, eternal life, protection
Lugh	Craftsmanship, healing
Mars	Aggression, vitality, courage
Mercury	Intelligence, communication, trade, travel
Mithras	Strength, virility, courage, wisdom
Odin	Knowledge, prophesy
Shiva	Destruction, transformation
Thoth	Knowledge, science, the arts
Tyr	Law, athletics
Vishnu	Preservation, stability
Zeus	Authority, justice, abundance

Personalized Magick and Ritualistic Witches

One commonality that Witches and Wiccans share is that both approach magick in personal ways—ways that can be incredibly complex or very simple. Kitchen Wiccans and Hedge Witches, for example, rely heavily on pragmatic, uncomplicated magick, much of which originates in folklore and superstition. Hedge Witches traditionally do not belong to a coven (a group of thirteen Witches; see Chapter 15 for more information on covens). Solitary practitioners depend on self-study, insight, creativity, and intuition as their main guideposts. Hedge Witches may be self-dedicated, but they are rarely publicly initiated. Similar to village shamans and cunning folk, they provide spells and potions for daily needs.

Some Witches practice magick with more ritualistic overtones, drawing inspiration from the Kabbalah (Jewish mysticism and magick) and other mystical and spiritual movements. Ritualistic Witches, for instance, approach every aspect of a spell as if it were part of a huge puzzle: Each piece needs to be in the right place for everything to work as it should. For example, the astrological phase of the moon should be suited to the task, and every part of the working should be carefully constructed to build energy toward a desired goal. Workings such as these have been used for a long time and are honored as part of the tradition from which the Witch originates. That is not to say that a ritualistic school has no room for variety or improvisation. It's just that the improvisation usually happens within a set framework.

Are You a Good Witch or a Bad Witch?

What's the answer to this classic question? Are there "bad" Witches who use their knowledge and power for personal gain and ill will? Yes, of course there are, just as there are "bad" Christians, "bad" Muslims, and so on. If you shake any figurative tree hard enough, a couple of rotten apples are bound to fall. That's just human nature. The good news is that these rotten apples are the exception, not the rule.

Just like everyone else, Witches confront issues that require them to make ethical choices. For instance, should magick be used as a weapon, even if it's only to fight back? Wiccans and Witches alike see magick as gathered from the life energy in all things. That energy is then turned and directed by the Witch toward a goal. It's how each person uses magick that makes it white (positive, constructive, helpful), black (negative, destructive, harmful), or gray (not completely black or white). Defining these things in concrete terms isn't easy, however, because each person's perception of what constitutes white, black, and gray isn't always the same.

The Wiccan Creed and the Threefold Law

White Witches (those who abide by a simple code that instructs them to work for the good of all) follow certain general guidelines. As the leading Neo-Pagan author Starhawk writes in *The Spiral Dance*, "Love for life in all its forms is the basic ethic of Witchcraft. Witches are bound to honor and respect all living things, and to serve the life force." This code includes:

1. Preserving the environment.
2. Honoring yourself and others.
3. Seeing sexuality as "numinous and sacred," part of the life force.
4. Understanding "What you send, three times over." This "Three-fold Law" basically translates to what goes around comes around, not just once, but three times! This is good reason to make sure your motivations are positive.
5. Knowing that we have the right to control our bodies.
6. Honoring the Goddess. As Starhawk writes, "The Goddess has infinite aspects and thousands of names—She is the reality behind many metaphors. She is reality, the manifest deity, omnipresent in all life, in each of us."

White Witches believe it's highly unethical to attempt to manipulate another person's free will with magick. This kind of manipulation occurs most commonly in love magick, if one person tries to force another's attentions. The problems inherent in this practice are obvious—a Witch who casts a love spell will always wonder if the object of her affection truly loves her, or if it's just the magick! In any case, this type of spell is selfish; it is certainly not cast for the good of all.

You won't find any spells in this book that harm anyone or anything. Remember, the Threefold Rule holds true especially for spells that seek to harm another.

With a spell, you're attempting to stack the odds in your favor—or in another person's favor. You're attempting to influence something in the future. We do this constantly, of course, through the power of our beliefs, but when you cast a spell, you bring your full conscious and creative awareness to the process. So remember your mother's advice: Be kind to others and be kind to yourself.

To ensure ethical practice, many Witches use a universal motto in prayer, spellcraft, and ritual: "For the greatest good and it harm none." Magickal people recognize that while the human mind and spirit have unlimited potential, the ability to recognize all possible outcomes of their magick is not unlimited. Human beings are not omniscient, and sometimes good intentions lead to terrible results. The universal motto, therefore, acts as a request for higher (and wiser) powers to direct the magick toward the best possible outcome, so that energy is not inadvertently misdirected.

☀ Wiccan Wonderings: Where do Witches go when they die?

Christianity has heaven. Buddhism has Nirvana. Many Witches believe that their souls go to Summerland, a resting place before reincarnation into a new body, in an ongoing cycle of birth, life, death, and rebirth. Although the idea of reincarnation cannot be validated, many Witches seriously consider the karmic implications of their actions or inactions. Reincarnation and karma teach that the past affects the present, and the present affects the future—no matter what life cycle you are talking about!

Finally, both Witches and Wiccans believe in religious tolerance and respect every path as having potential for human enlightenment. Since people are different, it only stands to reason that the paths they choose to walk are different. In keeping with this outlook, you will never find a Witch or Wiccan standing on a street corner preaching about magick or faith. Both groups believe that people must choose their own path. In fact, by virtue of coming from other religious backgrounds, many Witches and Wiccans have done exactly that.

This brief overview is a broad generalization at best. Each Witch relies heavily on his or her inner voice or conscience in decision-making and in the way he or she wields magick. Witches believe that each person creates his or her own destiny by action, inaction, karma, and so on. There is no cut-and-dried answer to whether anyone is a good or a bad Witch, but most Witches hope to be the best Witches they can be!

Living and Thinking Globally

The worldview of most Witches bears striking similarity to those walking a Shamanic Path. Like shamans, they see the Earth as a living, breathing classroom to honor and protect, not a place to conquer and control. Every living thing in this world has a spirit, a unique energy pattern, including the planet itself. As a result, Witches tend to think globally, mindful of nature and the cosmic universe.

Earth as a Classroom

The Witch's body houses his or her soul. Since most Witches believe in reincarnation, their time on this planet is spent gaining and applying spiritual principles to stop the cycle of reincarnation eventually and return to the Source. Witches regard the Earth, its creatures, and its elements as teachers that have the power to reflect the divine plan and pattern that extends throughout the universe.

With this in mind, most Witches strive to weave their magick and live their lives within natural laws, working in partnership with the planet instead of fighting it. Many Witches are strong proponents of protecting endangered lands and wildlife, feeling that these losses not only eliminate a wonderful learning opportunity but also are a crime against Gaia (one name for the Earth's spirit; in Greek mythology, the Earth Goddess). Witches often send out positive energy from spells and rituals aimed at protecting a particular environment or species, or directed like a healing balm at the whole world.

✳ **Wiccan Wonderings: What should I do if someone important in my life is opposed to my spellcrafting?**
The best thing you can do is try to educate your loved one on what Wicca and Witchcraft really is and what it is not. Try to have an open dialogue about his or her concerns and your feelings about your practice. Perhaps he or she is operating under misconceptions about Wicca or spellcrafting that you can gently dispel with facts. However, arguing about it is the worst thing to do. If the person still chooses not to look past misconceptions, don't try to convince him.

Above and beyond caring for the environment, how else does this kind of global thinking affect Witches? Mostly in the way they perceive things. A rock, a flower, an herb, a tree, or a stray animal may all hold special meaning, depending on when and where it appears and what's going on in the life of that person. For example, if a wild rose suddenly grows in a Witch's yard, he or she might take it as a positive omen of love growing in the home. Taking this one step further, the clever Witch would thank nature for its gift, dry some of those petals, and turn this little treasure into love-inspiring incense!

A Word about Spellcasting

In the next chapter, you will learn some basics about what is necessary for casting spells. Always keep in mind that the most important elements in a spell are your intent and passion, not the words or the ritual. Once you have a grasp of the basics, you can design spells for any situation. Remember, when casting any spell, it's always wise to open with a prayer for protection of yourself and others. This prayer can be from a traditional religion or one that you create yourself. Make such a prayer your opening ritual.

The following Zen prayer is actually the first spell you're going to cast. This prayer, said for someone in need, is simple, powerful, and at least 2,500 years old. It's most effective when you say it without being attached to the outcome. By saying the prayer, you're acknowledging that a higher force is at work and that force or power knows what is best for the person for whom you're saying the prayer.

Think of this as a boost to the spiritual immune system—it increases a person's available energy. When you write it out, jot the name of the person for whom you're saying the prayer at the top.

May He Be . . .
May he be filled with loving kindness.
May he be well.
May he be peaceful and at ease.
May he be happy.

Chapter 2

Belief, Intent, and the Magickal World Around You

Snow White, Cinderella, The Wizard of Oz, Alice in Wonderland, Beauty and the Beast, Peter Pan, Star Wars. For most of us, these stories are where we first discovered spells and potions, Wizards and Witches, and the never-ending struggle between good and evil. Fairy tales showed us a world filled with magick—one where inanimate objects like mirrors, stones, and gems can have special powers; animals can talk; plants can think; and with a sprinkling of dust, kids can fly.

Then we, like Peter in the movie *Hook*, grew up and forgot about magick. Our lives became a little less rich and our imaginations started to shrivel as we got mired in the mundane details of our daily lives. Every now and then, we recapture some of that early magick through books and movies like *E.T.,* Lord of the Rings, and Harry Potter. But usually, we have to be reminded.

Belief is the core of any spell. Without it, all you have are words and gestures, light and dust, nothing but bluster—rather like the Wizard that Dorothy and her companions exposed to be just an ordinary man. But what, exactly, is meant by belief? Go back to Oz. The Lion sought courage because he believed he was cowardly. That belief ruled his life until the Wizard pointed out how courageous he actually was. The Lion realized that he had possessed what he desired most all along. Believing he didn't have courage is what crippled him.

✴ **Wiccan Wonderings: Are complicated spells better than simple spells?**
One isn't better or worse than the other. The complexity or simplicity of a spell should fit the situation and the desired result. If your life is busy and you're already pressed for free time, then simple spells may suit your lifestyle better than complicated rituals.

Most of us are just like the Cowardly Lion. Maybe, for instance, you want abundance. To you, maybe that means financial abundance, money in the bank, freedom from worrying about your debit card being declined. But to those around you, your life appears to be incredibly abundant—you have a loving family, wonderful friends, a job you love. Sometimes, a shift in your deepest beliefs happens because someone you love or whose opinion you respect points out that you actually have what you desire. Other times, you reach the same conclusion on your own. In either case, the end result is the same: Your beliefs shift, and ultimately, your reality changes.

The Power of Your Beliefs

A belief is an acceptance of something as true. In the 1400s, people believed the world was flat until Columbus proved otherwise. In the 1600s, men and women were burned at the stake because people in power believed they were Witches who consorted with the devil.

On a more personal level, each of us is surrounded by the consequences of our personal beliefs. Your experiences, the people around you, your personal and professional environments—every facet of your existence, in fact—is a faithful reflection of a belief.

Some common ingrained, limiting beliefs that people hold on to include:

- I'm not worthy (of love, wealth, a great job, whatever).
- I'm a victim. I can't do anything right.

- Happiness is what other people experience.
- People are out to get me.
- My health is bad.
- Money is the root of all evil.
- I can't do it (start a business, sell a book, whatever).
- I'm trapped.
- I'll never find the significant other who is right for me.
- I live in an unsafe world.

There are as many limiting beliefs as our imaginations can conjure. The foundations for many of these notions are laid in childhood, when we adopt the beliefs of our parents, teachers, and other authority figures. Childhood conditioning about beliefs can be immensely powerful. Inside the man or woman who lacks a sense of self-worth lurks a small child who may believe she's a sinner, untrustworthy, or not good enough.

On a larger scale, our beliefs are also gleaned from the cultures and societies in which we live. A woman living in the West, for example, won't have the same core beliefs about being female as a woman in, say, a Muslim country.

A belief system usually evolves over time. It's something that you grow into, as your needs and goals evolve and change. Even when you find a system of beliefs that works for you, you hone and fine-tune it, working your way deeper and deeper into its essential truth. Everything you experience, every thought you have, every desire, need, action, and reaction—everything you perceive with your senses goes into your personal databank and helps create the belief system that you hold in this instant. Nothing is lost or forgotten in your life.

You don't have to remain a victim of childhood conditioning. With will, intent, and passionate desire, you can define for yourself what you believe or don't believe, what you desire and don't desire.

Invisible Beliefs

Most of us have lots of "invisible beliefs." These are deeply rooted beliefs that are largely unconscious and often so powerful that despite our best intentions and conscious desires, we can't seem to make headway in accessing them. The challenge is to bring these beliefs into conscious awareness and work to change them, if necessary.

One of the best ways to identify these invisible beliefs is to take an honest look at the people and experiences in your personal life as though they were a mirror of the beliefs you hold. Does your boss continually overlook you when it comes to promotions? Do your coworkers ostracize you? If so, perhaps you have an invisible belief that you're not worthy. If you continually attract relationships riddled with problems and drama or you attract abusive relationships, then perhaps the deeper belief also has to do with your lack of self-worth.

If you don't like what's happening to you and would like to change certain elements in your life, try reflecting on what you believe in order to identify the beliefs that could be holding you back and the beliefs that are beneficial to your goals. Figure out which beliefs are really yours, as opposed to beliefs you learned from someone else and unconsciously adopted as your own.

If you're not sure about your belief system, the time to define it is before you begin casting spells—not after you've started. Once you know what you believe, it's easier to define your parameters, your boundaries, and the lengths you will go to attain something. It also helps in determining what you won't do, and establishing your bottom line.

Start by taking inventory of your life and writing down as many of your beliefs or preconceptions about yourself as you can. Zero in on your negative assumptions, and turn them into positive affirmations instead. By writing down the positive affirmation, saying it to yourself over and over during the day, and backing the affirmation with emotion, your unconscious will eventually begin to believe it. Once your unconscious believes it, the process of change and transformation begins to show up in what you experience.

Exercise: Describe Your Beliefs

In 200 words or fewer, describe your beliefs, your own personal code. If you're not sure about your belief system, simply list what you think you believe.

It's not always necessary to make radical changes in your life—although it always helps to make a physical gesture that affirms your new belief. Simply begin to question why you do certain things, and you'll start to uncover your invisible beliefs about yourself and about how life works.

Your Personal Code

Every magickal tradition, from the Druids to Wicca to Santería, has its own code—principles that guide the practitioner, boundaries that he or she won't cross, a core of beliefs that permeates everything he or she does. These core beliefs define the parameters of the magickal practice. In Wicca, the primary principle is to harm nothing and no one.

But individuals also develop their own personal codes. Have you defined yours? As previously noted, cultural differences have a hand in sculpting a particular individual's beliefs. In the end, however, each of us must refine our own code as we evolve from children raised in the belief systems of our parents to adults who decide for ourselves what we believe.

This is not to say that any of us is omnipotent, that any of us has all the answers or even a good chunk of them. We're all seekers and we all have a need for some sort of belief system.

Your belief system may include an adherence to an organized religion or to some other spiritual discipline, or it may not include any sort of spiritual ideas at all. But at the heart of any belief system lies a code by which you live your life, and it may not have any connection whatsoever to other people's concepts of good and bad. After all, even thieves have codes.

Do you believe in an afterlife? In a supreme being? In good and evil? Do you believe that reality is exactly as it appears, that what you see is what you get? Do you believe people can't be trusted, that all Dobermans are vicious, that it's every man for himself, that you're a victim and there's nothing you can do about it? Then your experiences will confirm those beliefs.

If, on the other hand, you believe that nothing is fated, that your free will and your innermost beliefs effect your reality, then your experiences will confirm that, too.

Because you have picked up a book on magick and spells, you probably already believe that you can shape your own destiny and are looking for practical information on how to do it more efficiently and pragmatically. Magick is one route. But there are hundreds of ways to get to where you want to be. The bottom line of any exploration is defining what you believe and what works for you.

Intent and Desire

The purpose of a spell is to manifest something that you need or desire. That need or desire (or both) comprises your intent. When you cast a spell, your intent is as vital to your success as your beliefs. What are you trying to accomplish? What's your goal? What outcome are you seeking? How badly do you want what you're trying to achieve or accomplish?

Defining your intent isn't difficult. Most of us do it all the time. On any given day, we make dozens of choices that manifest in any number of ways, and we do it without the ritual of casting a spell. We don't always recognize it, but our intent constantly creates magick in our lives. Despite our astonishment and delight when magick happens in our lives, we usually write it off as a mere coincidence and eventually forget about it.

Defining What You Want

This should be easy, but for many of us it's not. When you get right down to it, most of us know what we want right this instant, but don't have a clue about the bigger picture. We're mired in the trees and can't see the forest. As you're thinking about what it is you really want to accomplish with your spells, be honest and patient, and take your time. Remember, the universe is never in a rush.

As you read through and cast the spells in this book, refer back to the brainstorming you did earlier in this chapter. The first hint you'll get about whether your beliefs are changing will be apparent in the quality of your experiences and relationships. You might notice that people are reacting to you differently and your life is opening up in unexpected ways.

How the Natural World Fits In

If you are serious about using magick and spells, you need to get in touch with the natural world around you. Although our everyday experiences might make it feel as if our "natural world" is the world of computers, the Internet, and offices sealed against the elements, this isn't the case. It's the wind blowing through your hair as you take a walk by the light of a full moon. It's the birds that live by the lake nearby, the trees that your kids climb, the flowers and the herb garden that you plant during the summer. The natural world is just as natural as it ever was, except there's less of it than there was twenty-five years ago, and most of us don't make enough of a point to enjoy it.

Take the time to rediscover the natural rhythms around you and the way they affect the flow of your inner life. If you don't do this periodically, you'll burn out and start to feel out of sync with everything around you. You need time out to go within. These natural cycles that we seek when we take time out are vital to success when casting spells. As the saying goes, "timing is everything"—and that timing is tied to the lunar calendar.

Spells and Lunar Cycles

Every month, the moon goes through eight distinct phases. For the first two weeks of a given month, from new moon to full moon, the moon is waxing, or increasing in size. This is a good time for casting spells dealing with manifestation and expansion. From the full moon to the next new moon, a period of about two weeks, the moon is waning, or shrinking in size. This time is optimal for spells dealing with decrease.

Who, you ask, would want to cast spells to decrease something, when most of us are seeking abundance? But if, for instance, you want to decrease your responsibilities at work or at home, casting a spell during the waning moon makes a lot of sense. Likewise, if you're looking to streamline your life, decrease your debt, tie up the loose ends in a relationship that no longer satisfies you, or lose weight, these spells should all be done under the waning moon.

The new moon is the time to plant symbolic seeds that represent whatever you're trying to create in your life. This is the time to cast spells for launching a new business, diving into an artistic project, starting a new relationship, or trying to get pregnant.

In any given month when there are two new moons, the second one is called the Black Moon. It is considerably more powerful than a regular new moon, so any seeding spells you do under a Black Moon might manifest more quickly.

The Need for Gratitude

In spellcraft, as well as life in general, gratitude is one of the most valuable attributes you can develop. It's imperative to accept all the good things and the compliments that come your way with a gracious thank you. Realize that this is the universe acknowledging your special individuality. Gratitude is intrinsic to any spell, so always end your spells with an expression of thanks.

The full moon is generally considered the time of harvest, when you see the fruits of the seeds you planted at the new moon. It's the best time to concentrate on the culmination of those spells. If your intent and desire are strong enough, it's possible to see the results of your new moon spells by the subsequent full moon, a period of about two weeks. Or, you might not see results until several full moons later. But you will see results. Spells for healing and empowerment are best performed during a full moon.

The Blue Moon, the name for the second full moon in a given month, is a particularly powerful time for focusing on spells you did at the new moon.

The odd and wonderful thing about timing your spells according to the phases of the moon is that it makes you more aware of them. How many times have you gazed up at a slivered moon and wondered whether it was waxing or waning? Probably not very often. Once you begin casting spells, that will change. There may even be subtle differences in your body rhythms or fluctuations in your menstrual periods, your libido levels, your hormones, or the level of your intuition.

The moon, after all, is our closest celestial neighbor. It influences ocean tides and blood tides. It is intimately connected to the ancient worship of goddesses, to the Druids' rituals, and to Wiccan practices. In astrology, the moon represents the feminine, energy that is yin, the mother, and nurturing, emotion, and intuition. It is our most direct link to the collective unconscious. Once you find your lunar rhythms, you're able to tap your link to the Divine.

Darkness

Darkness is the time to cast spells, but forget the images you have of the three Witches in *Macbeth*, stirring their cauldron and cackling under the light of a Cheshire cat moon. Darkness in the real world isn't like that at all. For many of us, the moment when the sun goes down marks the beginning of the time we spend with the people we love, doing the things we love. In the modern world, darkness usually means the end of the work day, the cessation of light, and winding down (or up, if it's Friday). Unless you work late shifts, darkness is the time that belongs to you.

In a deeper sense, though, darkness marks a perceptual change. Our imaginations spring to life; we hear and see things that the noise and light of the day obscure; our intuition is sharper, more vivid. All of this adds to the mystery and wonder of all that is possible instead of confining us merely to what we think we know. In darkness, your beliefs shift more easily and often shift in bold, dramatic ways.

This doesn't mean that you can't cast spells during the daylight hours. The universe, after all, doesn't care when you make your wish. It's just that in darkness, it's easier to imagine what might be, and the capacity to imagine is integral to the success of any spell.

The Wheel of the Year

As you consider natural cycles, it's important to look at what happens over an entire year as well. For centuries, Earth-honoring cultures have

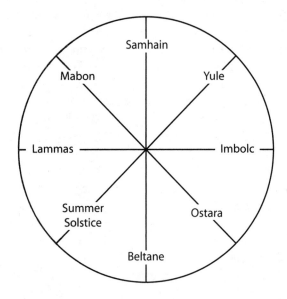

followed the sun's passage through the sky. Our ancestors divided the Wheel of the Year, as the sun's annual cycle is known, into eight periods of approximately six weeks, with each spoke corresponding to a particular degree in the zodiac wheel.

In Wicca and other Pagan belief systems, these eight holidays (or holy days) are called sabbats. It's no coincidence that many modern-day holidays fall close to these ancient solar dates and are still celebrated in similar ways. Each of these special days affords unique opportunities for performing magick spells and rituals.

Samhain

The most holy and solemn of the sabbats, Samhain (pronounced *SOWeen*) is observed on the night of October 31. It is a time to remember and honor loved ones who have passed over to the other side, hence Halloween's association with the dead. Also known as the Witches' New Year, Samhain begins the Wheel of the Year.

Wearing costumes on Halloween stems from the early practice of making wishes on this date (similar to New Year's resolutions). The colorful custom of dressing up as the person you'd like to be in the coming year serves as a powerful magick spell and visual affirmation. Magicians believe the veil that separates the seen and unseen worlds is thinnest on Samhain. Therefore, this is an ideal time to try to connect with nonphysical entities such as ancestors, angels, or spirit guides. Many people also do divination on Samhain, when insights and information flow easily.

Winter Solstice or Yule

The Winter Solstice occurs when the sun reaches 0 degrees of Capricorn, the shortest day of the year in the Northern Hemisphere, usually around December 21. In pre-Christian Europe and Britain, the joyful holiday celebrated the birth of the Sun King, who brought light into the world during the darkest time of all. It's easy to see parallels between this ancient view and the Christmas story.

Putting up an evergreen tree symbolizes the triumph of life over death, for these plants retain their needles even during the cold winter months. Traditionally, a Yule log is burned on the eve of the Winter Solstice. Ashes from the Yule fire are collected and used in magick charms to bring blessings in the months ahead.

Imbolc, Brigid's Day, or Candlemas

This holiday honors Brigid, the beloved Celtic goddess of healing, smithcraft, and poetry. The sabbat is celebrated either on February 1 or around February 5, when the sun reaches 15 degrees of Aquarius.

Imbolc means "in the belly," and the holiday honors creativity in its many diverse forms. Brigid is known as the lady of the flame or hearth, so fire plays a prominent role in the festivities that mark her special day. Sometimes she is depicted with a cauldron, which represents the womb and the receptive, fertile quality of feminine energy. At Brigid's Day rituals, participants may build a fire in a cauldron and drop requests written on slips of paper into the flames. Often candles are lit in her honor, each representing a wish or intention a celebrant hopes that Brigid will bring to fruition.

Spring Equinox or Ostara

Usually celebrated around March 21, the Spring Equinox occurs when the sun enters 0 degrees of Aries. This sabbat recognizes one of two dates each year when daylight and night are of equal length. Thus the holiday celebrates a time of balance, equality, and harmony.

The first day of spring, Ostara is a fertility holiday, a time for planting seeds—literally or figuratively—that you want to bear fruit in the coming months. This is an ideal time to launch new ventures or begin a new relationship. The word *Easter* derives from Ostara, and the custom of painting eggs (symbols of fertility and promise) has its roots in this sabbat.

Beltane

Beltane is usually celebrated on May 1, although some people prefer to mark it around May 5, when the sun reaches 15 degrees of Taurus. The second fertility holiday, Beltane coincides with a period of fruitfulness, when flowers blossom and new life emerges. The Maypole, around which young women dance, is an obvious phallic symbol.

In early agrarian cultures, celebrants built fires on Beltane and led livestock between them to symbolically bless them and increase their fertility. Human couples, too, saw Beltane as an auspicious time to express creativity, sensuality, and fertility. Beltane rituals often included sexual activity, and children conceived on this date were said to belong to the Goddess. Whether you wish to spark creativity of the mind or body, Beltane is an ideal time to cast spells for growth and abundance.

Summer Solstice or Midsummer

The longest day of the year in the Northern Hemisphere, the Summer Solstice generally occurs around June 21, when the sun enters the zodiac sign Cancer. To agrarian cultures, this was a time of plenty, when crops were ripening and winter's barrenness seemed far away. They celebrated this joyful holiday with feasting and revelry.

The symbolic seeds you planted earlier in the year now begin to bear fruit, too. This is a good time to collect herbs and flowers to make good-luck charms, especially those designed to attract abundance. Remember to give thanks on this holiday for the riches you've already received.

Lughnassadh or Lammas

Named for the Celtic god Lugh, this holiday is marked on August 1 or around August 5, when the sun reaches 15 degrees of Leo. Lughnassadh (pronounced *LOO-na-saad*) is the first of the harvest celebrations. Farmers cut grain at this time for baking bread and brewing beer.

Pagans today still enjoy sharing bread and beer with friends on this sabbat. While you're kneading the bread, add a dried bean to the dough. The person who gets the bean in his or her piece of bread will be granted a wish before the next turn of the wheel. Remember to share your bounty with the nature spirits who helped produce the harvest—leave some food out for them as a gesture of thanks.

Autumn Equinox or Mabon

The second harvest festival, the Autumn Equinox usually falls around September 22, when the sun moves to 0 degrees of Libra. Day and night are now equal in length, so this sabbat represents a time of balance and harmony.

Early Pagans fashioned a doll from corn, wheat, or straw to represent the Sun King, whose powers are waning, and tossed it into a fire as an offering to Mother Earth. You might also choose to braid three stalks of grain together, each stalk symbolizing a wish that you want to come true. Hang the braid in your home to remind you of your intentions.

The Days of the Week

In astrology, the days of the week are governed by particular planets, and the planets have specific meanings. In order to tip the odds in your favor, it's always good to align the type of spell you're doing to the most propitious day of the week.

The Days and Their Rulers

Day	Ruler	Meaning
Sunday	Sun	Success, healing, happiness
Monday	Moon	Intuition, women, mother figure, creativity
Tuesday	Mars	Energy, passion, sexuality, aggression
Wednesday	Mercury	Communication, messages, the mind, the intellect, siblings
Thursday	Jupiter	Expansion, luck, success, higher education, the law
Friday	Venus	Love, art, beauty, money, women
Saturday	Saturn	Responsibility, structure, details

Common Concerns about Spellwork

Once you've assessed your own belief system and considered it in the context of natural rhythms and cycles, you can begin delving into some of the more logistical aspects of casting spells. Before you do that, let's clarify a few common concerns about spellcrafting.

First off, yes, spells do often work, but there are certain instances when they don't. For one thing, you can't force another person to do something that isn't in alignment with his or her highest good. You can curse, hex, or cast spells on someone to fall in love with you until you're blue in the face. But if loving you doesn't align with that person's highest good, nothing is going to happen.

✳ **Wiccan Wonderings: How often should a particular spell be done?**
Always give your first spell a reasonable amount of time to work—several days to a month. A spell that is in alignment with your highest good, and backed by intent, clarity, and passion, can work immediately. For a complex spell that involves several people, the spell may take longer. Give it at least a month if it's complicated and a couple of weeks otherwise. Or, break the complex spell down into its components and simplify it.

If a spell doesn't work, it might also be because your intent isn't strong and clear enough, or you haven't put 100 percent of your emotions behind it. Not to mention that we sometimes wish for things that aren't in our best interest. A spell is never going to work if what you want isn't in your highest good.

But who or what determines what is in your—or anyone's—highest good? That answer goes by different names: the higher self, the soul, the grander self, All That Is, the Goddess, God . . . . Whatever you call it, the central idea is that when you look in the mirror, the reflected image is a fraction of the whole picture. Somewhere in each of us is something, some type of energy, that grasps the whole picture.

Much of the time, we lose sight of things as our lives get bogged down in the details. According to esoteric thought, however, each of us has a blueprint of our lives, a kind of master plan, that we designed before we were born. We set up certain events and encounters to provide the types of experiences that would help us evolve. Whether we keep these appointments with destiny is up to us, and that's where free will comes in.

If you've applied the above criteria and your spell still isn't working, then perhaps you're asking for too many things. You should determine what's most important to you, then ask for just that. Sometimes, just rearranging the wording of a spell fixes the problem.

Also be sure to re-evaluate your goal, and any accompanying spells, if it changes. Even if your goal has remained the same, you could try the spell again, but with renewed passion and greater clarity about what you want. The more passion and emotion you put behind a spell, the greater the chances that it will work quickly.

Remember not to invest too much energy in the outcome of a spell. Once you cast your spell, forget about it. Release it, then let the process unfold. Trust that you'll get what you want. Casting spells is meant to be done in a spirit of fun and adventure. If your spells don't seem to be working, take a closer look at your mood. Are you approaching it too seriously? If so, then lighten up.

Chapter 3

Creating Sacred Space

Buddha once said, "Wherever you live is your temple if you treat it like one." Most Witches and Wiccans would agree. Sacredness is more a matter of attitude and behavior than it is of trappings, and it certainly requires no building or props. Nonetheless, creating a sacred space to practice magick is important, and there are tools and processes Wiccans use to create magickally safe havens for their efforts.

In Wicca and Witchcraft, spells are often performed in a Circle, and group work, especially gatherings in which there are public rituals, frequently takes place in a circular "sacred space." A Circle shows that each person present is important to the success of the overall working. The Circle also represents unity, accord, wholeness, and a safe psychic sphere within which all can find comfort and protection.

Power Spots

Before you cast a Circle, you need to find your own power spot, because where you do your magick is as personal as the kind of magick you do. Some people prefer a specific spot that remains intact from the casting of one spell to the casting of the next. Others have no such loyalties and move their spot around—the yard one night, the garage the next. Find the spot that feels most comfortable and gives you some privacy if you live with other people or have pets. Cats are especially curious about anything new going on where they live.

Interior Places

Some people favor power spots with a minimum of furniture and things, others like being surrounded with objects that remind them of magick and enchantment. It's up to you. If you're going to be casting a Circle for your spells, find a spot that's large enough to do so. Create an atmosphere that is calm and peaceful, and remove anything distracting or noisy that might disturb that atmosphere. It helps to cast spells in an area with a pastel floor and walls. If the floor in your space is tiled or wood, find a throw rug or pillow that complements or matches the colors of the walls. You can also use it to sit on during your magickal work.

In addition to a throw rug, pillow, or something else to sit on, you'll need a surface of some kind on which to work and put things. It can be as casual as a wooden box or a board propped up by bricks, or as ornate as an altar (you'll learn how to build your own altar in sections to follow). It's all a matter of personal preference. If the surface is used for other purposes, smudge it (burn sage and allow the smoke to suffuse the area) before you use it.

If you have a favorite object—a statue, a stone, a crystal, or anything else—keep it in the area where you cast your spells. Consider it the guardian at the gates, a power object that will maintain the magickal atmosphere even when you're not there. You might want to use a small object, so you can move it easily. That way, your magickal atmosphere will travel with you. Even if you don't have a spot that's perfect, don't lose any sleep over it. Simply bring your intent, passion, and belief to any spell you cast, and you'll be on the right track.

Outside Locations

Finding a power spot in nature requires some time and intuition. Even if you decide to cast spells in your backyard, you still need to find a spot that feels right. You can do this by walking the yard or the area you've chosen elsewhere and being alert to any unusual or intense body sensations: heat, cold, a chill, a cozy warmth in the pit of your stomach. Listen to those sensations, and you'll know which spot is right for you.

Dowsing is another way to find the right spot. Dowsing was originally used to locate water. The idea is to use a forked stick or some other tool to sense the location of whatever you're looking for, so it dips down to pinpoint the best location. Use the forked branch of a willow, if you can find one, or make a dowsing rod from wire hangers. For any dowsing tool to work, though, it should be infused with your intent and purpose. Request aloud that the dowsing rod locate the right spot for your spellcasting.

Creating the Proper Ambiance

The casting of a protected, sacred space keeps out unwanted spiritual influences, purges the air of negative vibrations, and instills a sense of positive purity. The sphere of energy around this space also holds any magick created within it firmly in place until the practitioners are ready to release and guide the magick outward. The time spent creating sacred space is an important psychological ally for the participants, allowing them to adjust their thoughts and attune them to matters of Spirit rather than flesh. That attitude is important to the success of even the simplest magickal process.

Only a focused Witch can harness the energy to enact the intended effects, so creating a successful sacred space means having the right overall surroundings for whatever is going to take place. The following guidelines will help you create the right ambiance for your sacred space:

1. Ensure you (or the group) won't be interrupted.
2. Choose the right space for your task, taking into account weather, personal time, or physical constraints, and what's going to take place in the sacred space once it's created.
3. Make sure the area is safe and tidy; get rid of anything that will distract you from the task at hand.
4. Set up your tools so they're readily accessible.

5. If you light candles, make sure they are not a fire hazard. Keep them away from flammable materials (like curtains).

Casting Your Circle

Since ancient times, circles have symbolized both power and protection. When you cast a Circle, you're working on several levels simultaneously. On a physical level you're defining the boundaries for your work, and on a spiritual level you're imbuing the space with your personal power. In *The Spiral Dance*, Starhawk describes the Circle as "the creation of a sacred space . . . Power, the subtle force that shapes reality, is raised through chanting or dancing and may be directed through a symbol or visualization. With the raising of the cone of power comes ecstasy, which may then lead to a trance state in which visions are seen and insights gained."

The Circle, then, is intended to contain the power you conjure. As in any magickal work, you bring your beliefs with you into the Circle. If you believe in demons or evil forces, then your Circle also serves as a protective device, a wall between you and whatever you perceive to be evil. It's important to feel comfortable and protected before spellcasting. Try to explore your beliefs and fear of evil forces before you cast any spell. Above all, know that you are in control and put your faith in knowing that inside the Circle, you are protected.

Your Circle should be large enough to accommodate the number of people who will be working inside of it, any objects that will be in the Circle, and your work surface. It should be cast clockwise, so that when it's completed you'll be inside of it. Make sure you have a compass with you—you'll use it to determine the four cardinal points, covered later.

✳ **Wiccan Wonderings: Must a Circle be cast each time a spell is done?**
In some magickal traditions, the casting of the Circle is such an integral part of a spell that not doing so is the equivalent of, well, heresy! Nevertheless, do what feels comfortable. Some people enjoy the ritual of casting a Circle or have a belief that urges them to do so. But if this

ritual doesn't appeal to you, or your beliefs tell you it's appropriate to do a spell without casting a Circle, then that's fine.

The Circle may or may not be visible in any magickal working. It all depends on the practitioner and the overall goal of the ritual or spell. Sometimes the boundaries are set directionally by words and actions alone. Other times functional altars mark the four quarters to honor the powers there. (The four quarters are the four main compass points of the working space; you'll learn more on this in sections to follow.)

In ritual magick, the Circle may actually be drawn on the floor. Some people use flour to cast the Circle; others use sea salt. In the absence of either of these, dirt, chalk, stones, brick, or a moat of water will serve the same purpose.

The substance you use to draw the Circle is less important than the inner feelings and concentration you bring to the act. Remember: Everything in spellcasting is symbolic. When defining the boundary of a sacred space, the item used to create the physical perimeter should match the theme or goal of the magick to be worked. A Witch working a love-oriented spell, for instance, might release rose petals between each altar point.

The Elements

The four elements are intrinsic to casting a Circle and to magick in general. They have magickal properties, just like anything else you'll use in spellcasting, and they act as conduits of your will. The following chart provides a simplified guideline to those properties:

Elements and Their Correspondences

Element	Direction	Color	Object	Quality
Air	East	White	Incense	Expression, communication
Fire	South	Red	Burner	Passion, initiative, energy
Water	West	Blue	Cup	Emotion, intuition
Earth	North	Black, green	Bowl	Grounding, stability, security

When you cast your Circle, you can locate the cardinal points with a compass, then mark them with any of the items listed in the "object" column or with a candle of the appropriate color. You can also use any other objects that are personally meaningful and represent that element. Improvise, and have fun with it.

In the east corner, you might place a piece of aventurine or tin, a yellow candle, a feather, or frankincense and myrrh. Following clockwise around the outside of the Circle to the south corner is the fire altar, which might house a piece of amber, a red candle, marigolds, or woodruff incense. In the west corner, suitable altar decorations might include a seashell, a blue or green candle, coral, vanilla incense, and a bundle of chamomile flowers. And in the north corner, you might use a potted plant, a green or brown candle, a piece of moss agate, and some patchouli incense.

Building an Altar

Most Witches include at least one central altar in a sacred space. Some Witches believe it's important to place their altars in the east, where the sun rises. For practical purposes, placing the altar in the middle of your Circle often makes more sense, especially if a number of people will participate in rituals in your Circle.

The altar provides a central focal point during spells and rituals. You can also display and store your magick tools here, especially the four primary items—the athame, pentagram, chalice, and wand (more on these later). You might consider decorating your altar with candles in attractive candleholders, flowers, statues of deities you feel close to, and crystals. Some Witches like to leave their magick tools out on their altars at all times; others prefer to store them when not in use.

Achieve Balance

If you choose to leave your ritual tools out on your altar, be sure to display all four principal items—athame, pentagram, chalice, and wand—together to establish balance. These four implements represent the four elements: air, earth, water, and fire respectively.

In addition to the four primary tools, you'll probably want to keep a variety of other magick items and ingredients on hand for your workings. Most Witches store a supply of candles in different colors, along with incense, essential oils, herbs, crystals, and gemstones. In time, you might also consider adding ribbons, parchment, small bags, a crystal ball, bells, a cauldron, tarot cards, runes, pendulum, ritual clothing and jewelry, and a Book of Shadows for recording your spells.

Some Witches change the decorations on their altars to coincide with the seasons and sabbats. This practice keeps your altar looking fresh and attractive, while also linking you to the Wheel of the Year and the cycles of life.

>>< **Wiccan Wonderings: Is an altar necessary for doing spellwork?**
Not necessarily—it's a matter of personal preference. If the presence of an altar troubles the people you live with or gets in the way, you can put the altar either in your own personal area or somewhere outside, if weather permits. If it seems too difficult to set up an altar space, simply don't have one.

How to Prepare

There are several ways you can prepare yourself for casting a Circle and all the magick to follow:

- Make sure you're well rested and mentally and physically healthy. Negative feelings undermine the success of any magickal effort.
- Take a ritual bath or shower before entering the Circle. This symbolizes washing away unwanted thoughts, tension, and energies. If this isn't possible, rinsing your hands in rose water (for perfect love) is a good alternative. Leave a bowl and towel near the entryway to your magickal area for this purpose.
- Dab your pulse points and third eye (located in the middle of your forehead) or the candles you plan to use with an oil that represents the purpose of your ritual or spell. For example, if you're

raising energy to improve a divinatory effort, choose jasmine or marigold—both enhance psychic abilities. This anointing acts as a magickal aromatherapy. (See more on incense, oils, and candles in Chapter 4.)

- Breathe deeply in through your nose and out through your mouth at least three times, evenly and slowly. Relax and release, making sure your mind and spirit are focused and centered, and your motivations are sound. This way, you won't be handling magickal tools and symbols with any lingering "bad" vibrations in your aura.

- Say a prayer. If you're working with a group, ask everyone to breathe together and join hands to unite wills and spirits before praying. The prayer doesn't need to be fancy, just sincere, to welcome Spirit as a helpmate to the magick you're about to create.

Calling the Quarters

Calling the quarters creates an invisible line of force that marks the space between two worlds—the mundane and the spiritual, the temporal and the magickal. This boundary usually begins in the east (where the sun rises) and ends in the west, creating a complete Circle around, above, and below the practitioner. The only time calling the quarters begins elsewhere is during banishing (when it often starts in the north and progresses counterclockwise to decrease negative energy), or when another quarter is more important or significant to the working.

For the sake of simplicity right now, stick with convention and begin in the east. Walk from the central altar to the eastern part of the Circle (or where you've placed the object or altar for that direction). Visualize a pure white light filling that space. As you walk the perimeter clockwise, continue visualizing this light shimmering outward, creating a three-dimensional boundary in your mind's eye. Some Witches find it helpful to trace this line with a wand or athame (see Chapter 4) to better direct the energy.

✳ **Wiccan Wonderings: What can be done inside a sacred space once it's created?**

Anything you wish. Read a spiritually inspiring book, meditate, pray, hold a ritual, weave a spell, or work on your Book of Shadows. Within this space, your soul can find a moment of calm and a sense of timelessness. All things are possible—just trust your heart.

As you arrive at each of the four directional points, recite an invocation, welcoming the elemental powers and asking them for protection and support. This following sample invocation begins in the east and proceeds clockwise around the space. It ends at the center altar with an invocation for Spirit. Note that the elemental energies of each quarter are honored in the words. If symbolic elemental items have been left at these four spots, they should be used somehow during the invocation (for example, lighting a candle to symbolize the presence of that power and to honor it).

East: Beings of Air, Guardians of the East, Breath of Transformation—Come! Be welcome in this sacred space. I/we ask that you stand firm to guard and protect, refresh and motivate. Support the magick created here by conveying my/our wishes on every wind as it reaches across the Earth.

South: Beings of Fire, Guardians of the South, Spark of Creation that banishes the darkness—Come! Be welcome in this sacred space. I/we ask that you stand firm to guard and protect, activate and fulfill. Support the magick created here by conveying my/our wishes to the sun, the stars, and every beam of light as it embraces the Earth.

West: Beings of Water, Guardians of the West, Rain of Inspiration—Come! Be welcome in this sacred space. I/we ask that you stand firm to guard and protect, heal and nurture. Support the magick created here by conveying my/our wishes to dewdrops and waves as they wash across the world.

North: Beings of Earth, Guardians of the North, Soils of Foundation—Come! Be welcome in this sacred space. I/we ask that you stand firm to guard and protect, mature and provide. Support the magick created here by conveying my/our wishes to every grain of sand, every bit of loam that is our world.

Center: Ancient One . . . the power that binds all the elements into oneness and source of my/our magick—Come! Be welcome in this sacred space. I/we ask that you stand firm to guard and protect, guide and fill all the energy created here. May it be for the good of all. So mote it be.

Releasing the Space

The more you work magick in an area, the more saturated with energy it becomes. Similarly, the more you invoke the quarters in that space, the more protective energy lingers therein. At the end of your workings, release the sphere you've created, thank the powers, ask them to keep guiding the energy you've raised, bid them farewell until the next time, then break the Circle. Breaking the Circle is a symbolic act that signals the completion of your magick. When you break the Circle, the Circle is "opened" and you step back into the ordinary world.

✳ Wiccan Wonderings: What is fire magick?

Fire magick is about enthusiasm, initiative, passion, and energy. Use fire magick when you're feeling lethargic or need to stir up enthusiasm. If you're in need of motivation, fire magick will help you get started. A burner is used when doing this sort of magick. Fire magick also includes candle magick and the magick of the sun (charging a crystal, for example).

Releasing the sacred space is effectively the reverse of erecting it. Begin in the north quarter and move counterclockwise (like you're unwinding something). Instead of envisioning the lines of force forming, see them slowly evaporating back into the void. Just because they leave your sacred space, it doesn't mean they're gone (energy can't be destroyed—it only changes form). They simply return to their source at the four corners of creation and attend to the tasks for which they were made.

As when casting the Circle, add a verbal element to provide closure. Words have very real power. The vibrations they put into the air clarify your understanding of what's happened in the sacred space and elicit evocative images that can dramatically change the outcome of your efforts. Try this sample invocation for releasing the Circle:

North: Guardians, Guides, and Ancestors of the North and Earth, I/we thank you for your presence and protection. Keep me/us rooted in your rich soil so my/our spirits grow steadily until I/we return to your protection again. Hail and farewell!

West: Guardians, Guides, and Ancestors of the West and Water, I/we thank you for your presence and protection. Keep me/us flowing ever toward wholeness in body, mind, and spirit until I/we return to your protection again. Hail and farewell!

South: Guardians, Guides, and Ancestors of the South and Fire, I/we thank you for your presence and protection. Keep your fires ever burning within my/our soul to light up any darkness and drive it away until I/we return to your protection again. Hail and farewell!

East: Guardians, Guides, and Ancestors of the East and Air, I/we thank you for your presence and protection. Keep your winds blowing fresh with ideas and hopefulness until I/we return to your protection again. Hail and farewell!

Center: Great Spirit, thank you for blessing this space. I/we know that a part of you is always with us, as a still small voice that guides and nurtures. Help me/us to listen to that voice, to trust it, and trust in my/our magick. Merry meet, merry part, and merry meet again.

The Sacred Space of Self

Now and then, there just isn't time to create formalized sacred space. Many Witches overcome this temporal challenge by accepting the idea that each person is a sacred space unto himself or herself. When time or space is lacking, the clever Witch simply uses visualization (often that of a white-light bubble) to provide herself with sacred sanctuary.

✳ **Wiccan Wonderings: What is air magick?**

Air magick involves expression and communication. The most powerful air magick you can perform is finding your magick word—the single word that resonates so deeply inside you that you can feel it racing through your bones. Once you find the word, you can use it to focus your personal power during magickal practice, or even to mitigate stress and anxiety anywhere, at any time. Burn incense when doing air magick.

Another alternative is to have four items that symbolize the four elements. Each of these items should be cleansed, blessed, designated for its function, charged, and then placed near its directional point. You can quickly activate a sacred space simply by envisioning the four objects connected by a line of energy, or by offering a shortened invocation and pointing to those spots in the room. Your invocation can be as simple as the following phrase:

Earth, Air, Fire, and Water—hear the words of my heart; protection and power impart!

Bear in mind that abbreviated castings like this can be just as powerful and functional as the long versions, as long as the Witch maintains a respectful demeanor, focus, and intention.

Chapter 4

The Witch's Kit: Tools and Symbolism

Now that you know how to find your own sacred space and cast your Circle, it's time to familiarize yourself with some of the tools you'll need for spellcraft. The tools of the Craft speak to your subconscious mind in forms that help support magickal workings. Witches and Wiccans will tell you that tools are good helpmates to magick, but they are not necessary to the success of any spell or ritual. A tool is only a focus, something to distract you from yourself. Without the Witch's will and directed energy, the potential in any tool will remain dormant. For example, a Witch might talk about quartz crystals as having energy-enhancing power, but until a crystal is charged and activated, that ability "sleeps" within. In magick, the Witch is the enabler. A focused will is all that any effective Witch needs for magick. Everything else just makes the job easier.

Charging Magickal Tools

It doesn't matter whether you make your own tools or purchase them ready-made. What's important is that you "charge" them before you use them for magickal work. Until you charge your chalice, it's just a goblet. The practice of charging it imbues it with your own energy and consecrates it for magickal purposes.

A charging ritual may be very simple or very complex—it's your choice. One easy and popular technique for charging your tools calls upon the four elements, again in symbolic form. First, wash the tool to cleanse it of any ambient vibrations. Next, hold your tool in front of you and visualize your energy flowing into it. Sprinkle the tool with saltwater and say aloud:

I charge you with water and earth.

Then hold it for a few moments in the smoke of burning incense while saying:

I charge you with fire and air.

Some Witches design rituals that involve the element to which the individual tool corresponds. You could charge your chalice by submerging it in a sacred pool of water for nine days. Similarly, you could bury a pentagram in the ground beneath a venerable tree or place your wand in the sunshine to let the sun's rays charge it. If you live near an ocean and find shells that are whole and nearly perfect, you can also charge these power objects by washing them in saltwater and putting them out into the sun for a while. If you wish, you can include music, crystals, or essential oils in the ritual. Be creative—engage your imagination and your emotions in the process.

Caring for Magickal Tools
Although some Witches display their tools on their altars, most people recommend storing tools in a safe place, such as a trunk or chest, when you're not using them. Wrap them in silk to protect them from dust, dirt, and ambient vibrations. If you drink wine or another beverage from your chalice during a ritual, of course you'll want to wash it before putting it away. However, there's no need to wash your other tools after

using them—the more you handle them and do magick with them, the more you imprint them with your energy.

Don't use your magick tools for mundane purposes. Use a regular kitchen knife, not your athame, for cutting food and herbs; drink everyday beverages from an ordinary glass, not your ritual chalice. Reserve these tools for spellworking and ceremonial occasions.

It's usually not a good idea to allow anyone else to handle your magick tools. If you work regularly with a magickal partner, however, you might make an exception for that person.

Book of Shadows

A Book of Shadows, also called a *grimoire,* is a journal in which you record your spells. It's a magician's secret diary and recipe file. Usually, you don't reveal your secrets to anyone else; however, you may choose to share them with a magick partner, members of your coven, or other people you trust.

Some grimoires are handsome, leather-bound volumes, while others are simple spiral notebooks. A loose-leaf binder that allows you to add and remove pages can be a convenient option. Decorate your grimoire in any way you like, with pictures, symbols, and so on. The point is to engage your imagination and personalize your book.

Stay Focused

Many people have trouble focusing their minds. Multitasking isn't a plus when you're doing magick. Because the mind is the most important tool in magickal work, you need to discipline your thoughts and learn to concentrate. Focused ideas and clear images generate better outcomes. If your mind keeps jumping about from one thing to another, you'll get mixed results.

Logging your spells in a Book of Shadows enables you to catalog your actions and results. Date your spells and rituals, as well as the outcomes you experience. Note astrological data such as the moon's phase and sign, the sun's position, and significant planetary patterns. Describe the situations or conditions in your life that are related to the spell, as they may influence what transpires. You might find it useful to jot down any feelings or thoughts you have while doing the spell, too. Over time, you'll probably update some spells as you discover which ingredients and procedures work best for you. As you become more proficient at magick, your spells and rituals may become more complex or specialized. Like a cook who's always expanding her culinary repertoire, you'll continue revising, improving, and adding new spells throughout your lifetime.

Athame

The origins of the word *athame* have been lost to history. Some speculate that it may have come from *The Clavicle of Solomon* (published in 1572), which refers to the knife as the Arthana (athame may be a subverted form of this term). Another theory is that athame comes from the Arabic word *al-dhamme* (bloodletter), a sacred knife in the Moorish tradition. In either case, there are magickal manuscripts dating to the 1200s that imply the use of ritual knives in magick (and special knives were certainly used in ancient offerings).

> ✳ **Wiccan Wonderings: What happens if a specific tool isn't available?**
> Find something else with appropriate symbolic value. For instance, some alternatives of an athame include a butter knife or wooden spoon (especially for a Kitchen Witch), a dirk (seen in Scottish Witchcraft), a sword (commonly seen in High Magick), or even a finger.

Modern Wiccans use the knife to represent the male aspect of the Divine and as a symbol of the will (both good and ill). Some Wiccans do not use their knives for anything other than spellcraft and ritual, while others feel that the more they use the tool, the more potent it becomes. There is also a strong belief that an athame used to physically harm another will never again be functional in magick, although in ancient times Witches often "fed" special knives with blood.

Other Alternatives

There are other tools that Witches might use instead of, or in conjunction with, an athame. Some of them include:

- **Labrys:** A double-headed ax that serves as a holy symbol for some Witches, particularly those who choose to follow Artemis or Rhea. The image of a labrys has strong connections with the Greek oracle at Delphi and, as such, is also suitable for anyone following Greek magickal traditions, in combination with or as a substitute for the pentagram (explained later in this chapter).
- **Staff:** An alternative to an athame or wand, used for directing energy. A staff may also be used like a sword in opening energy pathways.
- **Sword:** A High Magick alternative to an athame. Witches sometimes use swords to cut an energy pathway into and out of the sacred space once a Circle has been cast.
- **Wand or rod:** These tools have all the functions of an athame. The only difference is that sometimes wands and rods become divinatory tools when carved or painted symbolically and then tossed or cast onto a surface. Some wands, like witching wands (Y-shaped branches), are used to locate lost items or sources of water.

Broom and Cauldron

Modern Witches do not rely on their brooms for flying, nor do they use their cauldrons to make slimy, noxious concoctions. These tools do have a purpose in magickal spells and rituals, however.

Broom (Besom)

The besom is a long-handled tool with a bundle at one end once made from the broom plant, which grows plentifully on European heaths and sandy pastures. Known for its yellow flowers and angular branches, broom is ideal for bundling. Thus, the instrument made of the broom plant and a stick also came to be known as a broom.

The broom is present in the folklore of various countries and cultures. Since Roman times, it has been associated with feminine power and magick. Prior to childbirth, women used a broom to sweep the threshold of a house both for protection and to prepare the way for the new spirit to enter. Gypsy marriage rituals included jumping over a broomstick to ensure the couple's fertility; this ritual neatly marked the line between single and married life.

Cauldron

Wiccans use the cauldron for both symbolic and practical purposes. Cauldrons appear in many mythological accounts; for instance, Odin received wisdom and intuitiveness from a cauldron, and Celtic legend mentions a cauldron of regeneration for the Gods. These types of stories, found in a variety of cultures around the world, give us clues about the origins of the cauldron's modern symbolic value. Specifically, Witches see the cauldron as an emblem of the womb from which all life, and many other gifts, flow. The three-legged cauldron represents the threefold human and divine nature.

✳ **Wiccan Wonderings: What are cauldrons used for?**
Witches have many practical uses for cauldrons. For example, they may use a cauldron to cook magickal foods and to hold beverages. Additionally, the cauldron can be filled with fire, water, flowers, or other items at specific times of the year to honor the point in the Wheel of the Year that a festival or altar commemorates.

A brazier is a good alternative for a cauldron. The word *brazier* comes from a French term meaning "live coals." A brazier is a fire-safe container that can hold a small fire source or burning incense. Braziers are ideal for indoor rituals and spells where fire is a key component.

Other Ritualistic Tools

Additional ritualistic tools commonly used by Witches include aspergers, chalices, goblets, horns, and mirrors.

- **Asperger:** Any item used to sprinkle water in and around the sacred space. In Scotland, a freshly picked branch of heather, which adds a lovely aroma to the water, is often used. Feathers, flowers, leaves, and brooms are all items used for asperging, along with the Witch's handy fingertips!
- **Chalice or goblet:** A symbol of the feminine aspect of the Goddess (and sometimes used to represent the water element). The chalice can be used to make libations. For a symbolic enactment of libations, the Witch places the athame point-down in the cup to represent the power of creation that comes from uniting male and female energies.
- **Horn:** An alternative to a cup or goblet, often used among Witches who practice a Norse or Germanic tradition. A horn can also be used as a symbolic item. Place it on the altar during times of need to invoke the spirits of plenty. Musical horns can also be used to call the quarters or to mark the release of a spell (announcing the way for magick).
- **Mirror:** Another multifaceted tool that is usually used in spellcraft to deflect negativity or improve self-image. Mirrors also make wonderful (and handy) scrying surfaces. (Scrying is a type of divination used by Witches.) Mirrors are also commonly used by Witches who blend feng shui with their arts.

✳ **Wiccan Wonderings: What is water magick?**

Use water magick when you need to sharpen your intuition or boost your emotions. The ocean is ideal for water magick when doing love spells. If you don't live near the ocean, incorporate objects from the beach—stones, shells, and sand. Then imagine yourself on a beach somewhere, out in the warm sun. The cup represents water magick when casting spells. Fill your cup with water, wine, or any other liquid you can drink.

Emblems, Costumes, and Regalia

Beyond the basic tools, many Witches have certain personalized emblems and regalia they keep for specific spells and rituals.

- **Cords:** In addition to holding robes in place, cords can indicate a Witch's level of skill in a specific tradition or group. Exactly how this custom came into being is uncertain. It may connect with the umbilical cord, thereby symbolizing a Witch's connection to the Sacred Parent, or perhaps even the myth of Ariadne's thread leading Theseus safely out of the labyrinth (which is a metaphor for life). Historically, cords were used in spellcraft, especially knot magick in Egypt, Arabia, and Europe, and they continue to carry that role today.

- **Crosses:** An equidistant cross represents crossroads (an in-between place), the four corners of creation, the elemental powers, and the four quarters of the Sacred Circle. Some Witches prefer to wear the cross in lieu of a pentagram.

- **Crystals, metals, minerals, and shells:** Nearly all types of crystals, gems, metals, minerals, and shells have been categorized for their elemental and magickal correspondences. Many Witches keep crystals on their altars to generate or collect specific types of energy, carry stones as amulets and charms, and even make crystal elixirs to internalize a specific stone's attributes.

- **Masks:** These play a role in sympathetic magick, whereby a person "becomes" what the item represents in the sacred space. This provides an extrasensory dimension in ritual and helps improve the overall result.

- **Pentagram:** A symbol worn by many Witches to represent the harmony of the elements, Spirit, and the self working together to create magick. The pentagram is also sometimes employed as a protective ward in written form either on paper or on the floor of a ritual space. Without the Circle around it, the pentagram is known as a pentacle, Solomon's Seal, and the Witch's cross.

- **Poppets:** Typically, poppets are created in the image of a specific person or creature so sympathetic magick can be directed from a distance at the subject represented. (Poppets can also represent a situation.) For instance, if you were to make a poppet of a beloved pet and carefully wrap it in white cloth to protect it, the animal would then receive the benefit of that protection. Witches also use corn or wheat to make poppets that represent the "spirit" of the grain, and keep them at home to ensure luck, a good harvest, and ongoing protection. Since the maker has a strong emotional bond to the poppet and uses that bond to affect a person over a long distance, the poppet qualifies as a talisman as well (see the section on Magickal Jewelry near the end of this chapter for information on talismans).

- **Robes:** While some Witches practice skyclad (naked), robes and other accoutrements help Witches "dress for the occasion" by separating that particular time from everyday-life events. Additionally, many covens use special markings or colors to indicate different things, like the season or a person's level of achievement in the group.

✳ **Wiccan Wonderings: What are sigils?**

Sigils are symbols used for various purposes. For example, sigils can be astrological emblems or symbols for the Gods and Goddesses. In Witchcraft, they function similarly to runes. You can even design your own original symbols. One way to do this is to draw what's known as a sigil. Choose a word that conveys your intention, such as love, prosperity, or success. Configure the letters in the word so they form a picture. Use upper- or lowercase letters, script or block, or a combination. Draw the letters right-side up or upside down, backward or forward, large or small—whatever strikes your fancy. When you're finished, you'll have an image that nobody but you will recognize. Both the act of creating the sigil and its application are magickal acts, so remember to approach the process in the right frame of mind.

Key Ingredients for Spells

As any good cook will tell you, the key to great food lies in the ingredients and how they are combined. The same thing is true for spells. If the components are not measured correctly, if they are not added to the mix at the right time, if you don't give them enough time to "bake" properly, the magick goes awry. The magickal ingredients give flavor to the magick, and that has been the case throughout history.

So what constitutes a good spell component? Anything that's essential to the recipe—anything that builds the energy until it's just right. It's important for all the ingredients to mesh on a metaphysical level. Their energy needs both continuity and congruity. Of course, the Witch herself can be the key component of any spell, with but a word, a touch, or a wish!

The lists that follow are by no means comprehensive, but provide enough information so that you can eventually design your own spells. You don't need to run out and buy everything on these lists; select a few staples that seem to fit the kinds of spells you're interested in casting. As you become more proficient with spells, you'll compile your own lists of what you like to work with.

Aromatic Oils

Our sense of smell is so acutely connected to memory that a single scent can conjure virtually any detail and instantly take you back to various phases of your life. All it takes is the whiff of a certain perfume, of sea air, or of fresh-baked apple pie and a slew of memories surrounding the person who is, or was, the love of your life instantly ensues. So it's no surprise that aromatic oils are used rather extensively in love spells.

✳ **Wiccan Wonderings: Can oils be charged?**

Yes, you can charge the oils you use in spells just as you would a crystal or stone. Place your bottle of oil on the windowsill where light will spill over it. You can request particular things from the oil, or just say a general prayer. Let it charge for an hour, then use it.

Following is a list of essential oils. These oils aren't to be ingested. They are best used in aromatherapy burners or in ritual baths. When anointing a candle with an oil, as some spells call for, rub upward from the base toward the top of the candle.

Acacia: meditation, purification
Almond: vitality, energy booster
Basil: harmony
Bay: good for love spells, prophetic dreams
Bayberry: money spells
Cedar: instills courage; good for protection, money, prosperity
Clove: healing, love spells, increases sexual desire
Eucalyptus: healing
Frankincense: prosperity, protection, psychic awareness
Honeysuckle: mental clarity, money
Jasmine: love spells, meditation, to sweeten any situation
Lavender: healing, purification, love spells
Mint: money spells
Patchouli: love spells, protection, money spells
Rue: protection
Sage: cleansing, wisdom
Vervain: money spells, fertility
Ylang-ylang: aphrodisiac, love spells, increases sexual desire

Herbs

In addition to a stash of essential oils, you'll want to stock up on essential herbs.

Acacia: for meditation; to ward off evil; to attract money and love
Angelica: for temperance; to guard against evil
Anise: for protection: The seeds can be burned as a meditation incense; the scent of the fruit awakens energies needed in magickal practices.

Balm: soothes emotional pain; mitigates fears

Basil: balance, money, purification, divination

Bay: heals; purifies; good for divination, psychic development, and awareness

Burdock: purifies and cleanses; protection; psychic awareness; wards off negativity; aphrodisiac

Catnip: insight, love, happiness

Chamomile: to bless a person, thing, or place; for meditation; also a sleep aid; helps attract money

Cinnamon: good for love spells, purification

Cinquefoil: energy; memory stimulator; allows you to speak your mind; protection; eloquence in speech; aids in divination, healing, psychic dreams

Clove: to get rid of negativity; cleansing

Clover: heightens psychic awareness; love spells, luck

Daisy: attracts good luck; love divinations

Elder: protection, healing rituals

Foxglove: heightens sexuality

Frankincense: meditation, power, psychic visions; used mainly as incense

Garlic: personal protection; healing; to lift depression

Ginger: love, assistance for quick manifestation

Hawthorne: success, happiness, fertility, protection

Jasmine: peace, harmony; to sweeten a situation or person, attract money, induce prophetic dreams

Kava-kava: heightens psychic awareness; good luck; anti-anxiety

Laurel: for attaining success and victory

Lavender: healing, spiritual and psychic development, love spells

Mandrake: toxic, handle with care, do not burn or inhale—used in amulets for luck, protection, fertility; many ancient mystical properties

Marigold: love, healing, psychic awareness, marriage spells, success in legal matters

Marjoram: acceptance of major life changes

Mint: speeds up results in a spell; prosperity and healing; attracts money

Mugwort: as a tea, aids in divination, psychic development and awareness, and meditation; good for washing crystals

Myrrh: usually burned with frankincense for protection, healing, consecration

Nettle: mitigates thorny situations such as gossip and envy

Parsley: protection, calming effect, eases money problems, good for health spells

Rosemary: protection, love, health; improves memory

Rue: strengthens willpower; good for health; speeds recovery from illness and surgery; expels negativity

Sage: excellent for cleansing a place with negative vibes; protection, wisdom, mental clarity; attracts money

Sandalwood: protection, spiritual communication, conjuring of good spirits, healing

Skullcap: relaxation before magickal practices

Thyme: helps focus energy and is used to prepare oneself for magickal practice

Vervain: a favorite herb of the Druids; cleanses negative vibes; good for protection, general boost to the spirit; attracts riches; good for creativity, divination; used as an aphrodisiac

Willow: love, protection, conjuring of spirits, healing

Wormwood: poisonous if burned—facilitates spirit communication; good for love charms; enhances psychic ability

Yarrow: divination, love, protection; enhances psychic ability

Incense

Incense has numerous functions for Witches. First, specially prepared blends like cedar and myrrh clear the air of any unwanted energies. Second, the smoke carries wishes and prayers to the winds (in this case, the aromatic base should match the intention of the wish). Third, burning incense can represent either the fire or the air element in the sacred space.

Colors and Candles

Unless you're color blind, color is intrinsic to your world. Yet, most of us take colors for granted—until we take a moment to appreciate a particularly stunning sunset or marvel at the vivid hues in a painting.

Science has proven that colors have a particular vibration, a tone that touches us in a particular way. Blues, pale greens, and pinks are tranquil; that's why you find them in hospitals, waiting rooms, and the dentist's office. Red stimulates and energizes; that's why your favorite Chinese restaurant is predominantly red. Yellow and gold buoy our spirits.

The colors you use in casting spells are a vital ingredient in the power of the spell. Even if you know nothing about color or spells, you probably wouldn't use black to attract money because you intuitively know that green or gold fit much better when trying to attract prosperity, money, and abundance. Likewise, it isn't much of a stretch to figure out that pink represents love and red represents passion. You can incorporate particular colors into your spells when using cloths to cover your altar, quartz crystals, stones and gems, or candles.

Safety First

No matter what color candle you're burning or for what purpose, remember: Never leave lit candles unattended.

Candles, in fact, are an essential ingredient in many spells. They can be used as either the focus of the spell or as a component that sets the spell's overall mood and tone. When imbued with personal power, they provide a means for focusing attention, and they offer protection. Lighting a candle represents igniting energy; carving a candle indicates the intention of the user; and pinning a candle marks the melting spot at which the magick will be released (kind of like an X marking the spot on a treasure map).

The symbolic value of the candle goes further. The flame represents the element of fire, which in turn signifies inspiration, passion, energy, and cleansing. Spells that require a fire source as a focus or component can easily be cast with a candle instead of a full-blown bonfire.

In various ritual constructs, candles represent the individual's soul, the presence of Spirit, or any one of the elemental powers. Candles may also be used for scrying, as a spell focus or component, and as a way of shifting the overall ambiance of an area to something more magickal.

No matter the application, Witches will often choose the candle's color and aroma to match the theme of the magick being created. For example, a simple white candle adorns the altar to represent purity of spirit.

It's best to have candles in a variety of colors. The list below gives the basic meanings of colors used in spells.

Amber: psychic sensitivity

Black: removing hexes, protection, power, spirit contact and communication

Blue: element of water, dreams, protection, intuition, health

Brown: element of earth, physical objects, perseverance, stability, practicality

Gold: success, power, prosperity, healing energy, higher intuition

Green: element of earth, lady luck, healing, balance, money, fertility

Indigo: intuition, serenity, mental power

Lavender: spiritual and psychic development, divination, mediumship

Light blue: peace, clarity, soothing

Orange: balance, clearing the mind, healing, attracting what you need or want, confidence, success

Pink: health, love, friends

Purple: spiritual power and development, business matters, spiritual wisdom

Red: element of fire, passion and sexuality, energy, courage, enthusiasm, action

Royal blue: independence, insight, imagination
Silver: psychic development, beginnings, intuition, meditation
Violet: psychic development and awareness, intuition
White: understanding, clarity, peace, protection, truth, purity
Yellow: element of air, contracts, divination, mental clarity, creativity, happiness

Gemstones and Crystals

Stones have a long history in the practice of magick. Gems appeared on sacred altars across the world as offerings to the divinities, and they cropped up in global superstitions with a multitude of virtuous powers. Gems could heal, protect, inspire fertility, indicate the outcome of battles, and improve crop growth. Some historians and folklorists have even raised the possibility that the original intent for wearing jewelry was more strongly based on the talismanic quality of its gems than as mere decoration. In the distant past, crystals were just as valuable as gems, simply because of their gemlike qualities and their scarcity. Today, crystals are far less costly and much more available than gems.

Stones and crystals are generally used when you want or need to affect the deeper layers of reality. Like herbs and colors, each stone has a different magickal property. Just as a sculptor releases the form inherent in a stone, so does the magickal practitioner release the power of a particular stone. With the proper attitude, a piece of jade will work as well as an emerald.

The relationship you have with your stones will be unique to you. Some will feel exactly right for whatever issue or purpose you have in mind; others won't "speak" to you at all. If you're going to work with stones, try reading a book called *Gemisphere Luminary* by Michael Katz. Each chapter discusses a particular stone and covers its history, spiritual properties, and role in the evolving consciousness of man.

✳ **Wiccan Wonderings: What's the best way to store stones used for spells?**

Some people recommend keeping stones in a velvet or cloth bag, a wooden box, or a special place, and they warn against other people touching them. Somehow, though, this seems old-fashioned and superstitious. It's fine to keep your stones where they can be seen, touched, and enjoyed. Just cleanse them with saltwater and let them sit in the sunlight for a while before you use them for a particular purpose, in order to charge them.

The guidelines provided below for stones and their magickal properties are simply a place to begin. With time, you'll develop your own ideas about which stones to use for which spells.

> **Agate:** Those that look like eyes were used to protect from the evil eye curse (and can still be used for protective magick).
>
> **Amber:** Lore tells us that amber came from the tears of a setting sun, and as such it's still used as a solar/fire stone. Witches also use it in healing magick (to capture disease much as it did insects).
>
> **Amethyst:** A spiritual stone. It can be used for meditation, for enhancing and remembering dreams, for cultivating wisdom, for the development of psychic ability, and to attract success and prosperity. It also helps with self-control, business cunning, courage, and safety in battle. It ranges in color from deep purple to rose.
>
> **Apache tears:** This is a type of obsidian that many Witches carry for luck.
>
> **Aquamarine:** A gift of the Sea Goddess, this stone bears the power of the full moon and helps manifest harmony, bravery, intuitive awareness, clarity, and a stronger connection with our superconscious. It is also good for healing, aids in the creative process, awakens spirituality, and fosters awareness of other levels of reality.

Azurite: The blue color of this crystal makes it ideal for dream magick and overall harmony.

Beryl: A transparent to translucent glassy mineral, beryl is used to promote harmony in relationships, success with legal issues, and motivation. Transparent varieties of beryl in white, green, pink, blue, and yellow are valued as gems.

Bloodstone: Used for healing and to connect more deeply with planetary energy. Also used for wish fulfillment, success, understanding weather omens, and safeguarding health. It is especially lucky for those born under the astrological sign of Pisces.

Calcite: Comes in a lot of colors, giving it a variety of potential magickal applications. Its energy is suited to encouraging spiritual growth, inner healing, and improved focus.

Carbuncle: Blood red in color, legend tells that carbuncle forms from the eyes of dragons. Its magickal correspondences include insight, health, and intuitiveness.

Cat's eye: The visual impact of this stone gives it strong associations with vision, especially our inner sight. Superstition tells us that cat's eye manifests beauty, luck, and prosperity.

Chalcedony: Offers protection from evil, good fortune, and improved communication and attitudes. According to legend, Mohammed wore a ring with this stone set in it. Carnelian, a pale to deep or brownish red variety of chalcedony, provides extra protection.

Chrysocolla: This opaque, charcoal-colored stone banishes fear and re-establishes logical perspectives.

Citrine: A pale yellow variety of crystalline quartz, citrine is a great stone for banishing nightmares and improving psychic abilities.

Diamond: Used for bravery, strength, invulnerability, clarity, and devotion. Among Hindus, Arabs, and Persians, the diamond represents overall success. Lore recounts how diamonds were formed by a thunderbolt.

Emerald: Used for clairvoyance and divination, healing, and growth. The emerald supports magick for faith, foreknowledge, strengthening the conscious mind, and resourcefulness. When emerald is worn with aventurine, another green stone, the two supposedly work synergistically to rid the body of cancer.

Flourite: This crystalline stone seems to strengthen the conscious mind and thinking skills.

Garnet: This gem was used in the Middle Ages to protect the bearer from nightmares. Witches use garnet for devotion, good health, and kindness. Non-gemstone—quality garnet is also available.

Jade: Jade has long been used as an amulet to encourage prosperity, enhance beauty, and inspire harmony, love, longevity, and the proverbial "green thumb" for those with poor luck in gardening. Low-quality jade is widely available.

Jasper: Used by the ancient Egyptians, red jasper is good for love spells and to stir up passions. Brown jasper is excellent for healing purposes. The stone also comes in yellow and green, but is most often found in the reddish hues and with mixed, swirling colors throughout its surface.

Lapis lazuli: For opening psychic channels, improving magickal insights, happiness, and meditative focus; dealing with children; and stimulating the upper chakras. Some of the best lapis comes from Chile, where it's inexpensive and often carved into animal figures. Shamans there use it in their spiritual practices. The most coveted lapis is a deep bluish hue, with almost no white flecks in it.

Malachite: A light to dark greenish stone, malachite can be attached to a child's crib to improve sleep or be carried for protection, specifically to remain aware of any forthcoming dangers or problems.

Moldavite: Energizes psychic talent, quickens spiritual evolution. Although not necessarily used in magickal practices, many people who wear it claim it affects them in a positive manner. (Be sure to wear it hanging about level with your heart.) Moldavite is

regarded as an extraterrestrial stone because it resulted from a
meteor collision with the Earth nearly 15 million years ago. It fell
over the Moldau River valley in the Czech Republic. Legend says
that moldavite was the green stone in the Holy Grail.

Moonstone: Under the rule of the moon, this stone bears very
similar energy to the lunar sphere. Use magickally to motivate
foresight, psychism, inventiveness, and nurturing abilities, and
to enhance the vividness of dreams and dream recall. Great for
Cancerian individuals.

Obsidian: One of the favorite stones for scrying mirrors, and
sacred to the patroness of Witches, Hecate.

Onyx: For banishing and absorbing negative energy. Good for
grounding during magickal work. Helps break deeply ingrained
habits, whether physical or emotional. Wear onyx when facing
adversaries in figurative or literal battle.

Opal: For those born in October, opal is a luck stone that improves
memory.

Pearl: Pearls are sacred to Isis in Egypt and to Freya among the
Saxons; they are also a symbol of the Goddess, the moon, and
the water element. Pearls are suited to spells focused on love,
happiness, and prosperity.

Peridot (chrysolite): When set in gold, this gem turns away evil,
nightmares, and malevolent magick.

Quartz: An all-purpose magickal stone, quartz represents infinite
potential. The color of the quartz often varies its applications
(for instance, use rose quartz for friendship and love magick).

Rose quartz: For healing and balance, and to amplify psychic
energy. In magickal practices, quartz is often used in conjunction
with other stones or orbs for a particular effect.

Ruby: Considered the most excellent amulet for health, mental
clarity, and harmony. Also stimulates the emotions, passion, and
unconditional love.

Sapphire: Brings divine blessings, the ability to understand omens and signs, luck, success, improved meditative states, and devotion.

Tiger's eye: Self-confidence, the freedom to follow your own path. In Rome, soldiers carried these into battle for safety. In modern times, this yellowish brown stone appears in spells and rituals aimed at improved stamina, good fortune, and prosperity.

Tourmaline: While this stone has little in the way of known ancient usage, it comes in a variety of colors, offering Witches flexibility in its applications. Overall, tourmaline seems to balance energy.

Turquoise: Safety in travel, rain magick, visual acuity, strength in friendship, and improved awareness.

This is just a brief list of stones. Many others are used in magickal work and, over time, you can compile your own personal list as you learn which ones work best for particular spells.

✳ Wiccan Wonderings: What is earth magick?

Earth magick is great for money and prosperity spells. It's also about nature. If you're in need of earth magick, go camping or hiking, or get out into the fresh air and appreciate the natural beauty that surrounds you. The bowl that represents earth magick is often filled with rice, but you can fill your bowl with any food that is grown.

Metals and Minerals

A good portion of the correspondences for metals and minerals comes to us through alchemists, the medieval chemists who searched for gold and instead discovered many other substances and their properties. Alchemists believed that everything on this planet could be broken down into key elemental correspondences; they often worked during the waxing moon to improve the results of their studies. Take a look at the following list of metals and minerals to familiarize yourself with their magickal correspondences and traits.

Boji stone: A projective stone Witches use to inspire symmetry, peacefulness, and a sense of foundation.

Brass: Brass is a fire-oriented metal that exhibits energy similar to gold but on a gentler scale. It's popular in healing and prosperity magick.

Copper: The preferred metal for making witching wands, copper conducts energy and inspires health, balance, and good foundations.

Feldspar: This substance is made of aluminum silicate and other minerals. Egyptians used feldspar as a tonic for headaches and other minor ailments. Magickally, it's associated with love, fertility, and working with the fey.

Flint: Durability; protection from mischievous fairies.

Gold: The metal of the sun and the God aspect, gold confers strength, leadership, power, authority, and victory to the bearer.

Hematite: Pliny recommended this iron ore to attract positive energy and exude charm. The ancient writers put hematite under the rule of Mars, which would also give it the powers of protection and strength.

Iron: Strength, safety, protection from spirits. Some consider iron an antimagick metal, which is why Witches prefer not to cut magickal herbs with an iron knife.

Lead: Greeks inscribed pieces of lead with incantations and then used them as amulets to ward against negative charms and spells. Its weight provides it with symbolism for reconnecting to the earth (keeping one foot on the ground), having a firm anchor, and overall practicality. Lead can be poisonous; please use it with caution.

Lodestone: The magnetic quality of this stone makes it ideal for attracting overall good vibrations into the Witch's life. In particular, it's good for relationship magick.

Meteorites: Because they come from celestial realms, meteorites are good for meditation, and for directing your attention to your place in the greater scheme of things. Promotes astral projection and improves understanding of universal patterns.

Pyrite: Carry this to protect yourself from being fooled.

Salt: At one time this substance was so valued that it was used as currency (Rome). Today, Witches use salt or saltwater for consecrating items or the sacred space, for banishing, and for overall protective energies.

Serpentine: A greenish, brownish, or spotted mineral used as a protective stone, mostly health-oriented.

Silver: The metal of the moon and the Goddess, silver inspires insight, dreams, psychic awareness, and creativity.

Steel: Steel is typically used to protect the bearer from fairies, or to afford general protection (especially when made into a ring).

Tin: A lucky metal, especially if you put it in your shoe.

Plain Stones, Shells, and Fossils

In addition to gems, crystals, and minerals, there are other stones and stonelike objects that people have used in magick, and that modern Witches and Wiccans continue to use. Each carries a specific energy imprint that the Witch activates and directs for specific goals.

Coral: Red and pink coral are the preferred types for protecting children. Carry coral for wisdom, insight, and to connect with the water element or lunar energies.

Cross stone: Sometimes called a fairy cross, this is a gifting stone that (because of its shape) honors the four quarters and their corresponding elements.

Geode: The geode has the power to create a natural womb for energy, and is an ideal Goddess emblem.

Hag stone: Also known as a holey stone, it's a plain rock found near the water that has a hole going all the way through it. This stone stimulates health, luck, and blessings, and is considered the gift of the Sea Goddess.

Jet: This ancient fossilized bit of wood provides strength and courage, particularly in difficult situations.

Lava: Being born of fire, lava burns away sickness and negativity.

Petrified wood: If you can determine the tree from which a piece comes, this fossil's energies will be connected to that type of tree. More generically, petrified wood helps you honor cycles in your life and improves the longevity of beloved projects.

Pumice: This is a very light stone. Carry a piece of pumice when you wish to ease your burdens and make the road ahead a little less difficult.

Round stone: To discover a perfectly round stone is considered good fortune, so if you find one, keep it. It also represents the Sacred Circle.

Sand dollar: A gift from the sea, the sand dollar provides protective energy, especially of your personal resources and energies (note the natural pentagram design).

Shells: Another gift from the sea, shells help us reconnect with the ancient ocean mother. They're good charms for improving divinatory ability, for learning to "go with the flow," and for acquiring the ability to listen to the voice of Spirit.

Stalagmites and stalactites: Once carried for protection and male fertility, stalagmites produce upward-moving energy, while the energy of stalactites moves downward. Stalagmites and stalactites may be used as magickal symbols for increasing or banishing power, respectively.

White stone: Among the Celts, a white stone found adjacent to a holy well could help the bearer see fairies.

A Tarot Deck

Pronounced *tar-OH*, this illustrated deck of cards (usually numbering seventy-eight) dates back to medieval times or earlier. It can be used as a form of divination or as a guide to spiritual/personal growth. The following tables might be helpful if you use tarot cards in any of your spellwork.

Tarot Cards as Significators

Tarot Card	Person It Depicts
King of Wands	An adult* male born during Aries, Leo, or Sagittarius
King of Pentacles	An adult male born during Taurus, Virgo, or Capricorn
King of Cups	An adult male born during Cancer, Scorpio, or Pisces
King of Swords	An adult male born during Gemini, Libra, or Aquarius
Knight of Wands	A young male born during Aries, Leo, or Sagittarius
Knight of Pentacles	A young male born during Taurus, Virgo, or Capricorn
Knight of Cups	A young male born during Cancer, Scorpio, or Pisces
Knight of Swords	A young male born during Gemini, Libra, or Aquarius
Queen of Wands	An adult female born during Aries, Leo, or Sagittarius
Queen of Pentacles	An adult female born during Taurus, Virgo, or Capricorn
Queen of Cups	An adult female born during Cancer, Scorpio, or Pisces
Queen of Swords	An adult female born during Gemini, Libra, or Aquarius
Page of Wands	A young female born during Aries, Leo, or Sagittarius
Page of Pentacles	A young female born during Taurus, Virgo, or Capricorn
Page of Cups	A young female born during Cancer, Scorpio, or Pisces
Page of Swords	A young female born during Gemini, Libra, or Aquarius

* Usually "adult" means someone over the age of twenty-five.

Today, most people wear precious and semiprecious gems mainly for adornment. In the metaphysical community, jewelry that combines magick with beauty is highly prized. Many New Age jewelers, who understand the historical and mystical properties of gemstones, now fabricate elegant jewelry for ritual wear, healing, and talismanic purposes.

Tarot Cards for Spellworking

Suit/Number	Your Intentions
Wands	Career, success, action, leadership, courage, passion
Pentacles	Money, property, material goods, security, physical health, protection
Cups	Love, relationships, intuition, fertility, nurturing, creativity
Swords	Communication, ideas, intellect
Ace	To start something new
Two	For relationship/partnership issues
Three	To manifest something
Four	For stability or protection
Five	To stimulate change or movement
Six	For joint endeavors or resources
Seven	To encourage peace or heighten intuition
Eight	For strength, permanence, sincerity, or to finalize something
Nine	For good luck, expansion, or success
Ten	To promote abundance and fulfillment

Magickal Jewelry

The Connection Between Gems and Deities

Gemstones have long been associated with gods and goddesses. In many cultures, gems were considered to be suitable offerings to the deities, and stones were often placed on altars as sacred gifts. In earlier times, only royalty and religious leaders wore gemstones. You can still see vestiges of these ancient beliefs in the practice of kissing the pope's jeweled ring.

When you wear gemstones, they absorb your personal vibrations. Pearls, in particular, are known to be affected by the emotions of the person who wears them. When you're feeling happy, a pearl will glow with a lustrous sheen, but it turns cloudy when you're down in the dumps. If you choose to wear family jewels or antique pieces, be sure to wash them in advance, in order to rid them of any lingering energies from other people.

Amulets and Talismans

The custom of carrying magick amulets and talismans is ancient. The early Egyptians placed good-luck charms in the tombs of royalty to ensure safe passage into the world beyond. Ancient Greek soldiers carried amulets into battle to protect them. An amulet or talisman may be a single object that has special meaning for its owner or a combination of several items—gemstones, botanicals, magickal images, etc.—contained in a "charm bag" or "medicine pouch," designed for a specific purpose. The energies of the ingredients plus your belief in their magickal properties give the talisman or amulet its power.

Do-It-Yourself Amulets

You can fashion amulets or talismans for yourself or for someone else. Place the ingredients you've chosen for your amulet or talisman in a cloth or leather pouch and wear or carry it in your pocket. If you prefer, put the items in a wooden box and set it on your altar. It's usually best to fashion a talisman while the moon is waxing; amulets should be made during the waning moon.

A talisman is designed to attract something you desire: prosperity, love, success, happiness, etc. Gemstones and jewelry have long been favored as talismans. The Chinese, for example, prize jade and wear it to bring health, strength, and good fortune. Amulets are used to repel an undesired energy, condition, or entity.

Chapter 5

Types of Magick

You have already learned about the basic tenants of Witchcraft and some of the general methods and tools of spellcasting. Before you jump into using that knowledge to begin working with specific spells for particular purposes, let's first explore a few of the various types of Witchcraft commonly practiced. While this is by no means a comprehensive overview of all magickal traditions, it will give you an idea of the various ways in which Witches put their craft to use.

Elemental Magick: Earth, Air, Fire, and Water

The elements are the four primary substances encompassing creation (all physical matter). But there is also a spiritual component to the equation. Following the Wiccan saying "As above, so below," Witches believe that each earthly thing also has a presence and form of expression in the astral world. Consequently, each element (earth, air, fire, and water) has been given astrological, mineral, plant, mystical, and lunar correspondences, as well as specific magickal attributes and personalities.

Earth: The Solid Element

In the eyes of a Witch, earth is the home of humans and all other beings, as well as a storehouse for all kinds of spiritual lessons. The earth element resides in the northern quarter of creation. The magickal energies embodied by the earth element include patience, foundation, and harmony. Earth is the element in which the soul puts down roots so it can reach safely toward the heavens. Other traditional applications for the earth element include magick aimed at slow and steady progress, fertility, financial security, and overall abundance.

A good deal of earth's magickal symbolism is illustrated in global myths and superstitions. Nearly every tribal culture regarded earth in a maternal aspect. For example, there are Native American stories that tell us about how the soul waits for rebirth in the earth's womb (under the soil). Similarly, there are dozens of myths, including those of ancient Sumer and Guatemala, that describe humankind as being shaped from soil. According to the ancient Greeks, the heavens were born into existence from the womb of Gaia, the mother who oversees all the earth's abundance.

Many farming traditions include giving offerings of bread or mead to the soil to ensure a good crop. It is from this custom and various Roman planting rituals that Witches come by land and seed blessings today. In fact, soil was used as a component in many old spells. People buried symbolic items to banish something or to encourage growth. For example, to remove sickness, one healing spell instructs a sick person to spit in the soil and then cover that spot and walk away without looking back. To speed recovery from illness, patients were encouraged to grow health-promoting plants in the soil from their footprint.

Air: The Elusive Element

Air resides at the eastern quarter of creation. Spiritually and mundanely, air is the most elusive of the elements because it is invisible, intangible, and very moody. It can be gentle or fierce, damp or dry, and each of these moods has slightly different magickal connotations. For example, a damp wind combines the power of water and air to raise energy that motivates and nourishes. The air element is applicable to traditional spells and rituals such as transformation, magickal dreaming, contemplation, renewal, working with spirits (ghosts), communication, and movement.

The ancients believed that the wind is influenced and changed by the corner of creation in which it originates. This idea translated into magickal methods quite nicely. If a wind is blowing from the south, it can represent fire and is said to generate passion, warmth, or energy for spellcraft. Similarly, a wind moving from the west brings water energies; from the north, it brings earth energies; and from the east, it doubles the strength of the air element!

We see a fair amount of directional wind work in spellcraft. For example, always scatter components in a wind moving away from you to carry a message or to take away a problem. Magick for new projects is best worked with the "wind at your back," for good fortune. When trying to quell anger, opening a window to "air out" the negative energy has great symbolic value, and, of course, when a Witch needs a wind, he or she has but to whistle! This is an ability said to have been passed down through families of Witches for generations.

Fire: The Element of Clarity

Fire takes up the southern quarter of creation. Magically speaking, the fire element empowers spells and rituals focused on banishing negativity or fear, dramatic purification, purity, enlightenment, power, and keen vision (the ability to see in the darkness). Because of its warmth, fire represents our passions, emotions, kinship, and a gathering of people. It was around the fire that our earliest tribes gathered to cook, tell stories, and celebrate life.

✳ **Wiccan Wonderings: What is a Witch's power element?**

Each Witch has one element to which she most strongly responds, called a power element. By working with and tapping into that element, a Witch can energize herself and her magickal processes. Determine your power element by going to places where you can experience each element intimately and paying attention to your reactions. Once you determine which element energizes you, find ways to expose yourself to it more regularly, to refill your inner well.

In spellcraft and ritual, fire is generally used in one of the following ways. As the best source of light, fire is set up in a special way (usually without chemical additives) so its energy supports the gathering. Moreover, items are released to the fire either to destroy a type of energy or to release energy into the smoke (which in turn carries the desire to the winds).

Water: The Element of Movement

Magickally, water resides in the western part of creation. The magickal energies embodied by water include wellness, gentle transformations, movement, tenacity, abundance, and nurturing. Also, because the moon affects the tides, water has a lot of the same correspondences as the lunar sphere in its full phase for spell and ritual work.

A very popular application for water in spells and rituals is for healing and protection from sickness. According to European custom, dew gathered at dawn banishes illness, making it a good base for curative potions. Likewise, bathing in the water from a sacred well, dipping your hands into the ocean's water three times (then pouring it behind you so the sickness is likewise "behind" you), and releasing a token that represents your sickness to the waves are old spells that easily work in today's setting.

Spirit: The Fifth Element?

Spirit (also known as ether) isn't an element per se, but it is often included in a list of magickal elements as the fifth point of the pentagram. It's even harder to define than air. Spirit is the binding link between the four quarters of creation and thus the source of magick. Spirit resides within and without, around, above, and below all things. While we can experience earth, air, fire, and water directly with our temporal senses, Spirit is elusive and depends on both the Witch's faith and spiritual senses to be experienced.

In spells and rituals, Spirit usually comes into play if the Witch or Wiccan chooses to call upon a divine figure to bless and energize her magick. Alternatively, it can come into the equation if several devic (fairy) entities are being invoked and need to be able to work together. Spirit provides the medium in which any and all elements exist equally well.

Kitchen Witchery: Eat, Drink, and Make Magick

Kitchen magick (also known as hearth magick) is among the simplest schools of witchery and easily applies to many spiritual paths. Kitchen Witches are similar to Hedge Witches in their methods and outlooks. Although the Kitchen Witch may work alone or in an eclectic group, a Kitchen Witch definitely adheres to the keep-it-simple outlook. If something is available and contains the right symbolism, it's fair game for kitchen magick.

Functionality, Finesse, and Frugality

These are the keywords that describe a Kitchen Witch's approach to magick. Functionality, finesse, and frugality work hand in hand. If something is not functional, why expend time, money, and effort on it? With finesse, the Kitchen Witch brings personal flair and vision into every spell or ritual she performs. With frugality, the Kitchen Witch keeps magick affordable, enjoying a positive spiritual path without breaking the family budget. Looking to functionality, the Kitchen Witch considers every item in and around the house as having potential for magick.

Ingredients for Successful Kitchen Witchery

The basic components for successful kitchen magick are:

- **Simplicity:** This allows the Kitchen Witch to focus on the goal rather than the process.
- **Creativity:** This allows the Witch to see the spiritual potential in even the most mundane items.
- **Personalization:** This makes the practice meaningful, and it is the meaning that provides the most support for manifestation of the magick.

The Kitchen Witch's philosophy and focus begin and end at home. Wherever you live can function as your sacred space; what makes it "sacred" is how you treat it. Every item and action in the Kitchen Witch's life, from brewing coffee to brushing teeth, can be spiritual if she chooses it to be so.

The Folklore of Hearth Magick

Many Kitchen Witches look to folklore, superstitions, and old wives' tales for magickal ideas. A lot of magick resides in these old stories, and they are very easy to follow. For example, how often have you seen people toss spilled salt over their shoulder without a second thought? That practice comes from a superstition that tossing spilled salt over your shoulder keeps evil away, and it gives the Kitchen Witch food for thought: Why not use salt (a common table condiment) as part of her magick for protection?

Kitchen Magick in the Kitchen

Of course, the ultimate expression of kitchen magick begins in the kitchen. Here you can make foods, beverages, potions, and notions that fill and fulfill body, mind, and spirit. To accomplish this, first do a little practical decorating. Hunt up some aromatic potholders, Witchcraft-themed trivets and refrigerator magnets, a candle or two, maybe even God and Goddess salt and pepper shakers!

✳ **Wiccan Wonderings: What is a Witch's personality element?**

Besides a power element, each Witch has a personality element. Earth people are grounded, like stability, plan everything, and have little patience for procrastination or flights of fancy. Air people are gypsy spirits who hate to be restricted and enjoy adventure, long conversations, and risks. Fire people are passionate and energetic (sometimes to the point of burning out); they dislike wishy-washy types with no spine. Water people like to go with the flow; they are healers, motherly types, and nurturers with unnerving psychic insights.

Once the kitchen has a magickal feel, choose the tools for the job at hand: You can use a wooden spoon as a wand and a butter knife for an athame. These items are in your kitchen all the time, so they absorb your personal energy, and they maintain a congruity of symbolic value in your sacred space. You can use nearly anything that's handy and that has the right symbolism. Use slotted spoons to strain out negativity, a blender to whip up energy, a microwave to speed manifestation, and dish soap for cleansing or asperging.

Steps for Making Magick in the Kitchen

1. Set up the space so it reflects your magickal needs and goals.
2. Choose kitchen tools appropriate to the work.
3. Choose your ingredients to support the process; in other words, match the magickal meaning of the foods, spices, and beverages with your goals and intentions. Don't forget to consider color and numeric symbolism as well. (This is also a good time to invoke the magick Circle.)
4. Chant, incant, visualize, sing. Empower whatever you're creating while you're making it. Make sure you do this at the most propitious time. For example, chant over bread while it's rising so the energy may likewise rise.
5. Serve the food in a manner that represents the desired manifestation. If you're working for joy, pattern the blessed food on the plate so it looks like a smile.
6. Say a prayer before using or consuming the results.
7. Trust in the magick.

It doesn't matter whether you're creating edibles, beverages, or just mixing up spell components that come out of the sacred space of home. What matters is that the meaningfulness is there, and the symbolism works in your mind and heart.

Food for the Spirit

People all around the world make spiritually enriched foods. For example, the Japanese eat a special glutinous-rice dish on their birthdays for luck, much as Americans eat cake.

Let's say you're preparing food for Samhain (Halloween), a festival for the dead. You might begin with potato soup (potatoes have eyes with which to recognize the spiritual world, and they help keep us rooted in this realm). Next, try a bean side dish for protection and insight. Black-eyed peas would work especially well here. For more safety, season the beans with onion and garlic. And for dessert, why not an apple or pumpkin pie to reflect the harvest? If making apple pie, make sure to rub the apples first (to rub away any "evil"); for pumpkin pie, carve the pumpkin first to chase away malicious spirits!

Magickal Properties of Common Culinary Items

Many of the edibles and spices in your home have various magickal associations. Here is a brief alphabetized listing of some of the items in your kitchen and their correspondences:

Alfalfa sprouts: frugality, providence
Anise: love, enthusiasm
Bacon: financial prosperity
Banana: male fertility
Bay leaves: energy, health
Beef: grounding, abundance
Bread: kinship, sustenance
Carrot: vision, the God aspect
Celery: foundations, peace
Chicken: health, new beginnings
Coffee: conscious mind, alertness
Eggs: fertility, hope
Honey: creativity, joy, well-being
Lemon: cleansing, longevity, devotion
Mint: rejuvenation, money

Olive: peace, spirituality
Pineapple: hospitality, protection
Potato: healing, foundations, earth energy
Rice: blessings, fertility, weather magick (rain)
Thyme: fairy folk, health, romance
Vinegar: purification
Wine: celebration, happiness

Making House Candles

House candles are an important part of the Kitchen Witch's household repertoire. They honor the whole living space and represent the spirit of the entire house, including all past influences. The easiest approach is to make or use candles in fire-safe glass containers, which can be left burning for several hours at a time.

To make a candle, melt wax over a low flame. If you wish, you can add aromatic oils or very finely powdered herbs. This is also a good time to incant, chant, or pray, indicating your intentions in verbal form. Put the wick into the glass container, keeping it in place by tying it to a pencil that is placed horizontally over the top of the container and adding a small weight (like a crystal) to make sure that the wick hangs straight down at the bottom. Let the wax cool slightly; then pour it slowly into the container. Cool and use as desired. Just make sure that the spell for which the candle is used somehow supports the goal of household harmony and peace!

Once you have a house candle, all residents of the house should be present the first time you light it. Each person's energy should be incorporated, so the candle itself becomes a representative of unity, trust, and love.

Green Witchcraft

Throughout history, various herbal remedies thought to have magickal properties eventually became what is known today as Green Witchcraft.

The heart and soul of green magick is an intimate connection to, and appreciation of, nature. Green Witches consider every flower, leaf, blade of grass—yes, even weeds—alive and sacred, filled with magickal potential. Although it is somewhat connected with Wild Magick (the magickal properties of the animal kingdom discussed later in this chapter), Green Witchcraft is more focused on plants, flowers, trees, and herbs as a mainstay for components, symbols, and energy.

The tenets of Green Witchcraft are as numerous as the plants found on this planet. Some plants are recommended as helpmates to magick, while other plants seem to deter witchery. For example, rowan bound with red thread is one of the most popular antimagick charms. Or, to find immunity from the Witch's spells, carry marjoram flowers in your pocket. Plants that assist Witches include anise, which helps avoid the ire of an invoked spirit; eyebright or mugwort, which improves psychic awareness; or periwinkle, which increases the power of a Witch's magick.

Putting Belief Into Practice

The first step in practicing green magick is to reconnect with nature. You can't honor something with which you have no intimate connection. The Green Witch strives to work in partnership with her plants. To that end, the Green Witch's garden is organic, and her household is one of diligent recycling. Living this way expresses the Green Witch's reverence for nature's gifts and ethical considerations in a practical way that brings the Green Witchery into daily life.

A Green Witch brings her philosophies and ideals into daily life and spiritual pursuits in lots of ways, including gathering loosened leaves and petals for magickal components (or to use in potpourri) rather than harvesting them; using plant matter as charms, amulets, and talismans; and adding plant matter to incense.

Natural Elements and the Sacred Space

To include plants in your sacred space, simply consider the symbolic value of the plant and its elemental correspondence. A variety of plants may serve as markers for the four elemental quarters of the sacred space. By choosing an item with the appropriate elemental association and putting it in the appropriate quarter, you honor the watchtowers and support the energy of the sacred space. When using a living plant isn't possible, it is perfectly acceptable to use a decorative item or an aromatic made from the appropriate plant. The following list contains some common plants and their elemental associations:

- **Earth (north):** alfalfa sprouts, beets, corn, fern, honeysuckle, magnolia, peas, potatoes, turnips, vervain
- **Air (east):** anise, clover, dandelions, goldenrod, lavender, lily of the valley, marjoram, mint, parsley, pine
- **Fire (south):** basil, bay, cactus, carrots, chrysanthemum, dill, garlic, holly, juniper, marigold, onions, rosemary
- **Water (west):** aster, blackberries, catnip, cucumbers, daffodils, gardenias, geranium, iris, lettuce, roses, willow

A plant's elemental association should also come into play with the time of the year. In the spring, air-oriented plants might decorate the altar, followed by fire plants in the summer, water plants in the fall, and earth plants in the winter. Of course, this correspondence may change according to their magickal tradition and is sometimes dictated by location and weather patterns, so this is only a generalized example.

Plants can also be used in the sacred space to honor particular gods and goddesses. Plants suited to whichever divinity the Witch plans to invoke into the space are placed on the altar or around the Circle. If, for instance, a Witch is working with Hera, a bowl of apples and a vase of irises would be suitable.

The remaining applications come in the enacting of the ritual itself. A Witch might use plants for asperging the sacred space (a branch of heather or woodruff are two favorites), wear them as head-pieces (wreaths of flowers and vines), or incorporate plants into her spellcraft. The limits are set by the goals of magick and the Green Witch's eye for creativity.

Plant-Based Spells

Exactly how a plant participates in magick depends a lot on its symbolic value, the goal of the magick, and the spell construct the Witch devises. Typically, plants may be bundled, burned, buried, carried, floated, grown, or tossed to the winds as part of a spell.

- Bundling is typical of portable magick.
- Burning is a way of releasing a prayer or wish and sometimes is also used for banishing.
- Burying is used a lot in health-oriented spells.
- Carrying a plant is typically a type of charm or amulet.
- Floating can take energy away from or toward the Witch, depending on the water's direction.
- Growing supports progress and manifestation.
- Releasing plant matter to the winds carries the magick outward from the Witch.

For example, consider a daisy. The daisy often appears in spells for love or to encourage fair weather. To incorporate daisies into your own magick, you could bundle three flowers and carry them as a love charm. You could also burn dry daisy petals in incense for fair skies, or release them to wind or water to take your wishes for good companionship to the four quarters of creation.

Or, take pine as another illustration. Because of the heartiness of this tree, pine represents longevity, fertility, protection from evil, and peace. Witches also say that its aroma brings joy and prosperity. Carry pinecones with you to improve your outlook, or bury them around the home to safeguard it. Pine needles are excellent additions to dream pillows, helping to bring a peaceful night's rest.

Although these examples are limited, they provide a good foundation on which any Green Witch can build a spell repertoire using her favorite plants. Just one note: If you cannot grow your own plants, please make every effort to ensure that your components are organic—or at least very well washed. Chemical additives impede or dramatically change the magickal energies of any natural item.

Creature Craft

Although the days of animal sacrifice are long over for most Witches, animals have not disappeared from rituals and spells altogether. If your pet is a familiar, a tuft of fur taken from his or her grooming brush might be used in spells to improve the rapport between you. A found bird feather might be used on an altar to represent the air element or to disperse incense around the sacred space.

✳ **Wiccan Wonderings: What is a familiar?**
A familiar is a spiritually attuned creature to whom the Witch turns for insights into nature's lessons, and for help in magick.

Beyond these kinds of applications, small statues or images of animals sometimes become markers for sacred space, depending on the creature's elemental association. For example, a fish image might be placed in the west to represent the energies of water, whereas a lizard might be placed in the south for "fire" energies.

Additionally, some Witches carry the image of a creature as part of spells or charms with specific goals in mind. For instance, carrying a lion carving might be part of a spell for courage. If the carving is made from bloodstone, carnelian, or tiger's eye, all the better, because these stones have strong metaphysical associations with bravery.

Although using animal parts as offerings and spell components is no longer practiced, the power in each living creature (or its representation) has not been lost to modern Witchcraft. Other magickal uses of animals might include placing an image of an animal in the sacred space to represent the energy of a particular element, or enacting spells that protect beloved pets.

Animals as Messengers of Nature

Witches believe that the patterns and messages of the Divine exist in nature. The natural world is a wealth of knowledge that humans would do well to learn and integrate into their lives. Part of it is the knowledge of animals and their role in nature that Witches have relied on in their magick. There is a longstanding global tradition of animal magick that the modern Witch can tap into.

Wild Magick

The definition of Wild Magick is very broad. Essentially, the Wild Witch seeks to defend nature, deepen her understanding of the wild, use this understanding as a spiritual tool, and then educate others regarding the state of the earth and how to preserve it. That's a pretty big job, but one that many Witches, Wiccans, and Neo-Pagans embrace. Wild Magick deals specifically with those moments when the "wild" world touches our nine-to-five reality in intimate ways. Animals represent a big part of that picture, especially the Witch's pets and familiars. Try the following strategy, a type of "wild" divination that relies on reading signs: Observe your pet's behavior with visitors in your home. It might give you some insights about your visitors you wouldn't otherwise get on your own, perhaps because animal reactions are based on instinct.

Outside the home, Wild Magick transforms a bit, especially when you're in a natural environment. For example, if a Witch observes gulls circling above a group of fisherman with their daily catch, he might gather up a stray feather and add it to his power pouch, in order to inspire extended vision, especially when hunting (figuratively). This, too, is Wild Magick: taking a gift from nature and applying it positively to your spiritual life.

Incorporating Animal Elements Into Magick

Anyone who's read Shakespeare is familiar with the idea of using animal parts in magick: "Eye of newt and toe of frog, / Wool of bat and tongue of dog . . ." (*Macbeth*, Act IV, sc. 1). Where did this tradition come from? Quite simply, humans have always trusted animal spirits (and the spirits of plants and inanimate objects) for their powers. A Magus (the singular form of Magi) who needed courage looked to nature's blueprint and found a lion, whose heart may be carried or otherwise used in a spell (thus the phrase "heart of a lion"). When a Witch needed stealth, it made sense to use the chameleon's skin as a spell component. When he needed perspective, a variety of birds came to mind, and he might harvest the eye.

Over time things changed, however. Only animal parts found in nature and properly cleaned are fit to be used magickally in Witchcraft. Modern Witches honor nature and her needs in their methods; eco-consciousness is a top priority. Here's a brief list of animal components and applications you would likely find on a random walk in nature:

- **Antlers:** Sliced antler makes a very sturdy carving surface, and may be used in making a personal set of runes. Alternatively, antlers can be carried to honor Artemis, Cernunnos, and Bacchus, or used as virility charms.
- **Eggshells:** Traditionally, shells were buried or burned in healing spells (often after having been carried by the patient so the eggshells "absorbed" the illness). Eggshells also make a good womb symbol in which energy can be nurtured to maturity. Be sure to consider the color of the eggshell in the final application. For instance, use blue eggshells to nurture peace and joy.
- **Feathers:** Use feathers for divination, for moving incense around the sacred space, or as a spell component in magick directed toward liberation and release. They're also good for meditations in which you wish to connect with bird spirits or the air element.
- **Fur:** Tufts of fur can often be found on burrs or other prickly bushes. If you can determine the animal that lost the fur, you can apply the fur as a symbol of that creature and its attributes in spells and rituals. For example, a bit of rabbit fur would be a good component to put in your power pouch for abundance and fertility. (Any small pouch will do as a power pouch. Use it to

keep special items, like small stones given by friends and those that carry personal meaning.)

- **Nails:** Nails serve utilitarian purposes (for gathering food) as well as defensive ones—when in the clutches of a foe. With this in mind, animal nails could be carried as amulets and talismans for providence and safety.

- **Teeth:** One of the longest-lasting parts of any body, teeth have natural associations with longevity and durability. Furthermore, teeth affect the way a lot of creatures communicate, so use them in different communication spells, depending on the type of creature involved. For example, if you were going into a meeting where clever discourse was needed, carrying a fox tooth might be apt.

- **Whiskers:** According to an old bit of folklore, cat's whiskers that you find somewhere can be used in a wish-fulfilling spell. For this to work, burn the whisker and whisper a wish to the smoke. This spell might be accomplished with the whiskers of other animals too, like using a dog's whiskers to inspire devotion and constancy.

The Elemental Animal

Witches draw on animal symbolism to mark the sacred space. Specifically, they use animal images to denote the element of a quarter, to honor a god or goddess, or to illustrate the theme of a spell.

As with everything else on this planet, animals have particular elemental associations. These associations come out of the creature's environment and predominant behaviors. It's easy to see that fish are aligned with the water element, and therefore the western quarter. On the other hand, some animals have two common associations: A poisonous snake like an asp relates to both the earth and the fire element, because it dwells close to the soil but is also native to a sandy, hot environment and has a lethal bite.

Within the sacred space, any of the animals aligned with the energies of a specific quarter can watch over that quarter as an appropriate representative. The following list provides the animals that embody characteristics of the four elements, as well as their combinations.

Earth (north): bear, cow, deer, ferret, gopher, mole, mouse, rabbit, snake

Air (east): bat, most birds, butterfly, dragonfly, ladybug

Fire (south): desert creatures, lion, lizard, scorpion

Water (west): crab, duck, fish, seahorse, seal, whale

Water/air: dolphin, flying fish, seagull

Water/fire: electric eel

Fire/air: bee, wasp, other stinging insects

Earth/water: amphibians, beaver

Animal Imagery in Magick

Animal imagery may be used as a way of accenting a magickal working. Rituals for earth healing, for endangered species, for a sick pet, to connect with the Wild Magick within, and so forth, would all benefit from this type of visual cue. The key is to choose the right animals for the goal of the ritual or spell. For example, when casting a spell for a sick pet, the images should mirror that pet (use photographs or at least images of a similar breed).

Familiars

Many Witches choose to have a familiar—a spiritually attuned creature (who lives with or nearby the Witch) who offers the Witch insights into nature, and for help in magick. Today's familiars include cats, dogs, birds, bunnies, and even the stereotypical frog, but, really, any living creature with whom the Witch can have an ongoing relationship or rapport can fulfill the role of the familiar! Actually, the Witch doesn't necessarily choose this creature so much as the animal and the Witch seem to discover and bond with each other. No matter what kind of creature it might be, the familiar is no mere pet. The animal in question is the revealer of truths and a respected partner in every sense except being human!

If a Witch wishes to put out a call for a familiar, he usually does so through a spell or ritual. This ritual typically takes place outdoors, near the home. The Witch begins by creating sacred space, and then he meditates, prays, and places the request in the hands of nature. During the meditation the Witch visualizes the living space so the right creature can easily find its way to the door.

Spirit Animals and Totems

Spirit animals are similar to angelic guardians. These noncorporal beings guide, protect, and assist Witches in both the physical and the nonphysical worlds. Some people believe spirit animals once existed in physical bodies, but have now passed over to the spirit realm, where they continue to aid human beings.

It's What Inside That Counts

The Kahunas of Hawaii and Polynesia say that the spirits of animals live inside people. These spirit creatures endow human beings with special talents or skills that are in line with the animals' characteristics. For example, someone who has a spirit eagle inside him might possess keen eyesight. A graceful dancer might embody the spirit of a gazelle.

Witches believe that everyone has at least one spirit animal who acts as a guide and guardian throughout the person's entire life. (The term "animal" in this case is used to refer to birds, reptiles, and insects as well as mammals.) This lifelong spiritual companion is often called a totem animal.

Remain open to nature's voice and avoid anticipating what animal might be your own totem. In some cases, your totem may possess qualities similar to your own. A busy, hardworking Witch might have a bee or ant as a totem. In other cases, your totem might display traits you've repressed or rejected and need to reawaken within yourself.

Power Animals

At times, additional spirit animals may show up to help in certain circumstances. These creatures, frequently referred to as power animals, lend their special energies or qualities to you temporarily. If you must overcome a formidable obstacle, for instance, an elephant might come to you to offer its strength and tenacity.

Connecting with Your Animal Guides

Meeting a power animal or totem often takes place in a ritual setting. Or the animal spirit may reveal itself to you through a seemingly chance encounter with its physical counterpart. If you notice an animal you've never seen in your area before or in an unusual situation, it's probably significant. Sometimes a spirit animal will come to you in a dream, or through repeated sightings in a variety of media. If you are fiercely protecting and nourishing a pet project, for instance, you might suddenly start seeing pictures of bears in magazines, on television, and so on.

The Good and the Bad

An animal's symbolism corresponds to the whole creature, both its positive and negative aspects. The otter, for example, is playful, but it can also get nippy. A Witch with an otter totem, therefore, might have a biting sense of humor or take frolicking a bit too far.

You can also choose to meet spirit animals through a process called journeying. This visualization technique usually involves going into a light meditative trance and imagining you are tunneling into the earth, perhaps by entering a cave or following a tree's roots down deep into the ground. As you journey, mentally ask animal helpers to present themselves to you.

When an animal appears, ask it what it wants to tell you or offer to you. A deer might advise you to be gentle with yourself and others. A lion may bring you courage. Try to become one with the spirit animal and feel what it's like to be that animal. The more you can involve your senses, the better. Remember to thank the animal for its friendship and help, before saying goodbye and returning to your ordinary awareness.

Animal Messengers

Our ancestors' lives depended on interpreting nature's signs accurately. Early human beings were well versed in reading weather patterns, the ocean's tides, animal behavior, and so on. Today, most people have lost this ability. If you pay attention, however, you'll soon notice that the universe regularly sends you signs to help guide you along your path in life—it's a bit like relying on road signs along the highway.

One way your higher self speaks to you is through animal appearances. Whether you see a physical animal in the wild (or in an unlikely spot), come across an unexpected image of one, or meet one in a dream, consider the visitation a message. The more alert you are to animal messengers, the more likely they are to show up to aid you and the better your communication with your higher self will become.

The following list shows signs and omens that correspond to various animals:

Animal Signs and Omens

Ant	work, diligence; biting predicts a quarrel
Beetle	good fortune; the larger the beetle, the better your luck
Butterfly	transformation, change for the better
Cat	meeting a black cat brings improved fortune and freedom from troubles
Cricket	domestic bliss
Crow	wisdom, hidden knowledge, magick
Deer	swiftness, gentleness
Dog	something new on the horizon (unless it's a black dog, which predicts misfortune)
Eagle	examine a situation closely; keep your eyes open
Fish	abundance, fertility, the potential for miracles (note the specific type of fish and its condition for more insight)

Animal Signs and Omens

Fox	beginnings that get off on the wrong foot; a need for cleverness or craftiness
Frog	matters of love or health (the condition of the frog will tell you more)
Hare	be cautious
Horse	good news, perhaps involving travel, is forthcoming
Lamb	peace and harmony
Lion	authority, courage, ferocity (when necessary to defend something you love)
Lizard	disappointment or lack of closure
Monkey	playfulness or flattery (not always with good results)
Mouse	difficulties, often of a financial nature
Owl	wisdom, messages, and news; pay attention to your inner voice in reacting to these missives
Pig	worries; insensitivity
Snake	treachery and betrayal, or jealousy
Spider	fate's hand at work in something, creativity; you may be caught in a web of your own making
Tiger	courage, competence, tenacity
Toad	the death of this creature portends increased tension

You might choose to keep a journal of animal sightings (or include them in your Book of Shadows) and your impressions regarding them. Date the entries. Record what happens after the animal's appearance, to see if the future unfolded as foretold.

Part 2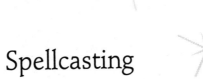

Spellcasting

Chapter 6

Spells for Love

Since this is the first of many chapters on spells for specific purposes, a note on what you can expect from your spells is in order. How quickly you get results from a spell depends, of course, on the clarity of your intent and your beliefs. If, in your heart of hearts, you really think this is all just mumbo-jumbo, then it's unlikely you'll see results. In that case, your time would be better spent working on changing that belief. On the other hand, if you're skeptical but open and receptive to the possibility that you live in a magickal universe and have the power to manifest what you need and desire, then you'll see results.

Sometimes when you do a spell, the situation seems to get worse before it gets better. This is possible with any kind of visualization exercise. Part of the reason is that when you consciously work with your beliefs and your intent, you're polarizing power within yourself, which helps rid you of negative beliefs. Once you're free of the negative beliefs, the situation improves.

The Truth about Casting Love Spells

Often, when we think of love spells, our minds conjure images of magickal incantations and mysterious potions meant to kindle the passions of a spellcrafter's otherwise indifferent object of affection. Fairy tales and Shakespeare aside, however, keep in mind that love spells aren't meant to enchant or bewitch someone into falling in love with you. We all have free will and nothing can violate that will—not even magick or spells. The true purpose of a love spell is to enhance and empower your own energy so you attract the individual who is the best for you.

Spells for love are numerous and varied, and before you do any, it's important to define what you want. Are you trying to attract someone? Looking for your soulmate? Hoping to enhance a relationship? The more specific you can be, the greater your chances of success.

Taking Emotional Inventory

Before you can fulfill your goals through spells, you first need to take inventory of your love life. The following questions should give you a fairly clear idea about the patterns that run throughout your intimate relationships. Once you identify your patterns, it's easier to change them.

1. Describe your ideal intimate relationship.
2. Describe the worst intimate relationship you ever had.
3. How would you rate your present sex life?
4. If you're involved, is your significant other romantic?
5. Are you romantic?
6. If you're involved, is your relationship emotionally satisfying?
7. What, if anything, would you change about this relationship?
8. If you're not involved, jot down five important things you're seeking in an intimate relationship.
9. Describe the most satisfying relationship you have now. It doesn't have to be romantic; it can be with anyone—a child, a parent, a friend, or even a pet.
10. Do your love relationships have a spiritual component?
11. List five things you would like to change about yourself, then five things you love about yourself.
12. List five things you admire about the person you love most.
13. List five things that make you feel good.

Loving Yourself

Loving yourself is a definite prerequisite for casting any love spell. It sounds simple enough, but so many of us have grown up believing that we aren't worthy, aren't attractive or intelligent enough, aren't this or that. Before you try any love spell, spend a little time uncovering your beliefs about yourself.

If you're holding on to negative beliefs about your worth as an individual, take a tip from author Louise Hay and adopt this simple yet powerful affirmation: "I love and approve of myself." Say it out loud, write it out, and post it on your mirrors, your fridge, and wherever else you will see it frequently. Yes, you probably will feel a bit foolish at first, but that just means the affirmation is working. When you repeat something often enough and back it with positive, uplifting emotion, your unconscious mind gets the message.

Putting Astrology to Good Use

In astrology, the days of the week are governed by particular planets and the planets have specific meanings. In order to tip the odds in your favor, it's always good to align the type of spell you're doing to the most propitious day of the week (see Chapter 2 for more on the meanings of each day of the week). Since these are love spells, they should be done on Venus's night, Friday, unless stated otherwise.

Another way to tip the scales in your favor when doing love spells is to use something that represents the other person's sun sign and element. If, for example, that person is a Taurus, you might want to enhance the earth element in your spell. Since water represents emotions and intuition, you could play up the water element, too.

Signs and Elements

Signs	Dates	Element
Aries	March 21–April 19	Fire
Taurus	April 20–May 20	Earth
Gemini	May 21–June 21	Air
Cancer	June 22–July 22	Water
Leo	July 23–August 22	Fire
Virgo	August 23–September 22	Earth
Libra	September 23–October 22	Air
Scorpio	October 23–November 21	Water
Sagittarius	November 22–December 21	Fire
Capricorn	December 22–January 19	Earth
Aquarius	January 20–February 18	Air
Pisces	February 19–March 20	Water

The Magickal Properties of the Sun Signs

These magickal properties can come in handy when casting spells for attracting love in general or a particular person.

Aries: Ruled by Mars, the God of war, you're a cardinal fire sign whose color is red.

Taurus: Ruled by Venus, Goddess of love and romance, you're a fixed earth sign. Your color is pale blue. However, some astrologers question Venus's rulership; they feel that Taurus is actually ruled by the earth. Consequently, shades of brown work with your sign, too.

Gemini: Ruled by Mercury, the messenger. As a mutable air sign, your colors are the pastels.

Cancer: Ruled by the moon, you're a cardinal water sign. Your color is the hue of the ocean or the pale luminosity of the moon.

Leo: Ruled by the sun, you're a fixed fire sign. Your color is yellow.

Virgo: Ruled by Mercury, you're a mutable earth sign. Your color lies in earth tones.

Libra: Ruled by Venus, you're a cardinal air sign. Pastels are your colors.

Scorpio: Ruled by Pluto, the God of the underworld, you're a fixed water sign. Your magickal colors are the deeper tones: navy blue, magenta, and olive green.

Sagittarius: Ruled by Jupiter, you're a mutable fire sign. Your magickal colors are hot and luminous: hot pink and burning yellow.

Capricorn: Ruled by Saturn, you're a cardinal earth sign. Your colors are earth tones.

Aquarius: Ruled by Uranus, you're a fixed air sign. Your colors fall in the pastels, like those of Gemini and Libra.

Pisces: Ruled by Neptune, God of the sea, you're a mutable water sign. Your colors fall in the vast spectrum of blues.

A Spell to Boost Your Confidence

As mentioned, the best way to get into the right frame of mind for love spells is to reinforce the love you have for yourself. This spell to boost confidence will help you remind yourself that you are worthy of love and that you *will* find it.

Tools:
Ylang-ylang oil
When: Whenever you need a spiritual or emotional boost

Set aside a few minutes when you won't be interrupted. Dab a couple of drops of the seductive ylang-ylang oil behind your ears and on the inside of your arms. Vividly imagine what is going to happen when you're with the person you're going to see. Hold the images in your mind as long as possible, maintaining the vividness and detail. Then release the images with the certainty that everything will come to pass as you have imagined.

A Simple Spell for Finding Love

This love spell requires only a handful of rose petals (preferably given to you by a friend or loved one so they're already filled with good energy).

Tools:
A couple handfuls of rose petals

Take them outside your house or apartment and scatter them on the walkway leading to your home, saying:

Love find your way,
Love come to stay!

Continue repeating the incantation until you reach your door. Retain one rose petal to carry with you as a love charm so love will follow you home.

A Spell to Attract a Lover

Tools:
A pink candle
Sandalwood oil
Lavender or your favorite oil

List of qualities
Pink pen
When: Friday, preferably around the new moon, definitely during a waxing moon

This spell requires some forethought, because you'll have to come up with a list of qualities you're looking for in a lover. Do you have certain physical characteristics or personality attributes in mind? Write your list in pink ink; be specific, but brief.

Then, on or around the new moon—or, at the very least, on a Friday night during the waxing moon, light your pink candle. Place your list next to the candle. Mix several drops of sandalwood oil, lavender oil (or your favorite oil) in your burner and light the candle inside of it. If the burner's candle is also pink, so much the better!

As the scent of the oil is released, imagine your lover. How does he or she look, act, and dress? What kind of car does this person drive? What type of work does he or she do? What are his or her passions? At the bottom of the list, draw the symbol for Venus: ♀.

Continue the visualization for as long as you need to make the mental images as vivid as possible. Inhale the scent of oils from the burner. Snuff out the candle's flames rather than blowing them out. At least twice between the time you perform the spell and the next full moon, mix your oils and light the pink candle and the candle in the burner. As the scent permeates the air you breathe, feel the presence of your lover. As always, express thanks.

On the full moon, release your wish by throwing away both candles.

A Spell to Find Your Soulmate

Tools:
A fresh rose
Rosewood oil
Ylang-ylang oil

A pink candle
A red candle
Empty glass container
When: On the new moon, preferably on a Friday

The red rose, which symbolizes the love you're looking for, should be placed in a vase of water on your altar. Put several drops of rosewood and ylang-ylang oil in your burner. Place the candles in a shallow ceramic or glass bowl. Light your oil burner. As you light the candles, say:

Winds of love, come to me,
Bring my soulmate, I decree.
This I wish, so mote it be.

Imagine yourself with your soulmate. Be as detailed and vivid as possible in your imagining. Pour emotion into this visualization. Feel the potentiality of attracting this person forming in the air around you. Let the candles burn all the way down, so the pink and red wax flow together in the shallow bowl. While the wax is still warm, shape it with your fingers so the pink and red are fully blended. Run cold water into the bowl so the wax doesn't stick, then remove the newly shaped pink and red wax, and place it near the door of your home.

On the night of the full moon, release the wax by tossing it out; also toss out the now dried rose.

✳ Wiccan Wonderings: Is there a magickal tool that's good for attracting love?

Love incense will empower you and help attract the person you desire. All you need is lavender, marigold, and rosemary. Charge the herbs under the light of the moon (several hours of exposure should be enough) before you grind them. Then sprinkle them over incense coal, which is available at most New Age bookstores or online. When you know you're going to be around the object of your affection, just light the incense beforehand.

A Tarot Love Spell

This spell is designed to draw the one you love closer to you using a tarot deck, which is available at most New Age bookstores or online.

> *Tools:*
> Deck of tarot cards
> Orange or lemon oil
> Pink, red, or orange candle
> *When:* During the waxing moon, preferably on a Friday when you're with the one you love

Choose whichever oil you like best (either one will do the job), and pick your candle color according to what you're trying to accomplish. Pink represents love, red represents passion, and orange represents balance.

During the waxing moon, before you're going to be with the one you love, put several drops of the oil you selected into your burner. Dip two fingers into the oil and anoint the candle with oil. Remove the suit of cups from your deck of tarot cards—it represents affairs of the heart. Then, select the king, queen, and nine of cups (the wish card). Place the three cards on your altar, between the candle and the burner.

Light the burner and your candle, and state your wish. Be specific. Imagine it happening. Blow the candles out when you're finished, anoint them again with the oil, and place them in the area where you and your lover will be spending time together. When the two of you are in that room, make sure these candles are burning.

On the night of the full moon, light the candles again, state your wish once more, then snuff out the flames rather than blowing them out. Throw out the candles when you're finished and give thanks.

Variations on Tarot Spells

One variation of the Tarot Love Spell is to select significators that represent you and the person you love. This method pegs the suits of the court cards to the elements. If you're a Gemini, for instance, and the one you love is a Sagittarius, then you would select a king or queen of swords to symbolize yourself and a king or queen of wands to represent the other person. If you're doing a love spell that involves younger people, you would use the pages of the appropriate suits. If you're doing a spell that involves a pet, use a knight of any suit that feels right to you. If you know your pet's sun sign, use the appropriate suit.

A Spell to Enhance Your Relationship

You're doing this spell on Thursday because it belongs to Jupiter, the planet that signifies expansion, success, and luck.

> *Tools:*
> A red candle
> A pink candle
> Sprig of rosemary
> Sprig of sage
> Abalone shell
> Object that represents the enhancement or expansion of the relationship
> *When:* A Thursday night during the waxing moon

Before you begin your spell, light a sprig of sage and smudge the room where you'll be working. ("Smudging" simply means moving the burning sage around the room so that its smoke passes over the walls and windows, the doorway, and your altar, purifying and cleansing the air.)

Place the pink and red candles at opposite ends of your altar, with the object that represents the expansion in the middle. With the sage still smoking, place it in the abalone shell. Add the sprig of rosemary to the shell. Now light the candles and the rosemary. Inhale the mixture of scents, shut your eyes, and imagine your relationship expanding in the way you want. Be detailed and make your visualization vivid.

Give thanks, then let the candles burn all the way down and throw them out.

✳ **Wiccan Wonderings: How do you determine with whom you're most compatible?**

In theory, the best match is someone whose moon sign is in your sun sign or vice versa. This would give you an instinctive understanding of each other. Another good match occurs when there are connections between sun, moon, and rising signs. The most passionate relationships often occur when the sign of your Venus matches another person's sun or moon sign.

A Spell for Personal Empowerment

This spell is particularly good when you're in a new relationship and are feeling somewhat uncertain or unsettled about where the relationship is headed. It's also good for any situation or time when you need to feel personally empowered.

Tools:
2 gold candles
Oil or sprig of frankincense
Sprig of sage
Deck of tarot cards
Pen and paper
When: The full moon

If at all possible, do this spell when and where the light of a full moon spills across your working area. Begin by lighting a sprig of sage to smudge the area where you'll be working and to increase your mental clarity. Next, remove the kings and queens from each of the four suits in your tarot deck.

If you're doing this spell for personal empowerment, simply select a king or a queen that represents the element of your astrological sign. (See the following chart for element correspondences.) If, for instance, you're an Aries, Leo, or Sagittarian female, then you would choose the queen of wands. If you're doing a spell that involves another person, then select a king or queen of the suit that represents the element of that person's astrological sign. If you don't know the person's sign, allow your intuition to guide you in your selection of a card.

On the sheet of paper, write out your intent. Keep it simple and specific. Place the paper on your altar, with the card or cards on top of it. Put one of the gold candles to the west, the other to the south. Light the candles and the frankincense. Shut your eyes and visualize what you desire. Then say:

Spirits of the west,
Clarify my love,
Spirits of the south,
Empower me.
So mote it be.

Give thanks, let the candles burn down, then toss them out the next day.

Tarot and the Elements

Suit	Element	Correspondence
Wands	Fire	Action, initiative
Swords	Air	Communication, intellect
Cups	Water	Emotions, intuition
Pentacles	Earth	Security, stability

A Spell to Turn Up the Heat

Has the spark gone out of your relationship? This spell uses spices to add spice to your love life, along with fire to heat up things between you and your partner.

Tools:
A fireplace, balefire pit, barbecue grill, hibachi, or other place
where you can light a fire safely
Matches or a lighter
A piece of paper
A pen that writes red ink
Cayenne pepper
Mustard seeds
Ginger
Jasmine
Rosemary
Bay leaves
When: During the waxing moon, preferably on a Tuesday

Safely build a small fire. On the paper, write what you find enticing
about your partner and what you desire from him or her. Be as descrip-
tive and explicit as you like—no one but you will read what you've
written. When you've finished, draw the runes Gebo, which looks like
an X, and Teiwaz, which looks like an arrow pointing up, around the
edges of the paper. These two symbols represent love and passion,
respectively.

Place the spices on the piece of paper and fold it to make a packet
that contains them. Visualize you and your lover in a passionate
embrace. As you hold this image in your mind, toss the packet of spices
into the fire. As it burns, your intention is released into the universe.

A Spell to Enhance Your Sex Life

Here's another spell that can improve your physical relationship with
your significant other. Do you two work such crazy hours that you
never have time for each other? Does your home always seem to be
filled with other people? Are your schedules so frantic that you both
constantly seem to be moving in opposite directions? If so, this spell
might be just the ticket.

Tools:
Ylang-ylang oil
Jasmine oil
4 red candles
Sea salt
When: Full moon or on a Tuesday, which is ruled by Mars (if not possible, a full moon on any day of the week works)

First, draw a bath and sprinkle sea salt into the water. Sea salt is an excellent psychic and spiritual cleanser. Soak as long as it takes to relax fully—not just your muscles, but down to your very cells.

When you're completely relaxed, dry off and put on loose and comfortable cotton clothing. If you have set up an altar, put several drops of both oils into an aromatherapy container. Light the candle beneath it. As soon as the fragrance begins to permeate the air, place a candle in each of the four directions, beginning in the north and moving clockwise. As you light each candle, say:

Goddesses of the north and south, the east and west,
Bestow your blessings, your power best,
On me and him (her) to make us one
It will be done.

When you're finished, put the candles, still lit, into the bedroom or wherever you and your significant other will be. Let them burn out on their own. Wipe out the oil container and add fresh drops of the ylang-ylang and jasmine oil. The candle under the container should be lit when you and your partner are together, so that the fragrance suffuses the room where you make love.

Intimacy Lotion

Does your lover seem distant lately? Is your sex life less fulfilling than usual? This magick lotion stimulates the senses to generate loving feelings between you and your partner and deepen your connection.

Tools:
A copper bowl
A silver spoon (silverplate is okay)
A glass or china container with a lid (ideally the container should be pink or red, and/or decorated with designs that represent love to you, such as roses or hearts)
Unscented massage oil or lotion
Essential oils of rose, jasmine, ylang-ylang, patchouli, and/or musk (choose the scents you like: one, two, or all of them)
When: During the waxing moon, preferably on a Friday

Wash the bowl, spoon, and container with mild soap and water. Pour the massage oil or lotion into the copper bowl. Add a few drops of one of the essential oils you've chosen. Using the silver spoon, stir the mixture, making three clockwise circles. Add a few drops of the second essential oil (if you've opted to include more than one). Again, make three clockwise circles to stir the blend. Repeat this process each time you add an essential oil. As you work, envision a beautiful pink light running from your heart to your lover's heart, growing to envelop you both in its radiant glow. When you've finished, pour the lotion/oil into the glass/china container and put the lid on.

Choose a time and place where you and your partner can spend an extended period of time together, undisturbed. Take turns massaging each other with the magick lotion. Relax and engage your senses. Allow the soothing touch and fragrant oils to enhance the connection between you.

A Spell for Keeping Promises

Your significant other keeps promising to take more time off work or clean out the garage. How can you transform talk into action? This spell gently nudges your partner to follow through on his or her promises.

Tools:
Essential oil of patchouli
A piece of agate
A tarot card that represents the promise you want your lover to keep—it should come from a deck you don't use for readings
When: During the full moon

Unless you're familiar with the tarot, you'll have to consult a good book on the subject to determine which card best symbolizes your situation. The knight of wands, for example, could represent an exciting trip; the eight of pentacles might be a good choice for financial matters. Sometimes the images on the cards will convey their meaning to you.

When you've chosen the card, put a drop of patchouli essential oil on each corner. Then lay the card face up on your altar, nightstand, or a windowsill in your bedroom. Set the agate on top of the card. Concentrate on the end result you seek—don't think about all the times your partner has let you down. Visualize the situation you desire clearly, as if it already exists.

Jealous Lover Spell

If your beloved overreacts whenever you look at or talk to someone else, or if jealousy, possessiveness, and mistrust are driving a wedge between you, this magick spell helps dispel envy and sweetens the situation.

Tools:
A ballpoint pen
A small pink pillar candle—not a dripless one
Jasmine essential oil

A heat-resistant glass, ceramic, or metal plate
Matches or a lighter
Dried white rose petals
Dried nettle
When: During the waning moon, preferably on a Friday, or when the sun and/or moon is in Libra

With the ballpoint pen, inscribe your lover's name on the candle; the candle represents him or her. Pour a little jasmine essential oil in your hand and coat the candle with it.

Set the candle on the plate and light it. Gaze at the candle and imagine you are looking at your partner. Explain your feelings and tell him or her how much you care, how important the relationship is to you. Reassure this person that you are trustworthy. Think only positive thoughts.

Allow the candle to burn down completely. While the melted wax is still warm, crumble the rose petals and the dried nettle. Sprinkle the botanicals on the wax. Then form the soft wax into the shape of a heart. Give the wax heart to your lover as a token of your affection and fidelity.

A Spell for Fidelity

Many spells dealing with fidelity and bringing home a wayward lover are manipulative in that they attempt to influence the other person. While these spells often work well, they can also backfire. This spell focuses on you rather than on the other individual. Just be sure of your motives if you're thinking of casting a spell for fidelity. Do you suspect that your significant other is being unfaithful? If so, do you really want to remain with that person?

Tools:
Sea salt
4 candles of the appropriate colors for the four cardinal points
Object that represents your lover

Object that represents you
Extra object to emphasize the water element (west)
When: During the full moon

Before you cast your Circle, make sure you have the objects you've selected on your working surface. Use sea salt to cast your Circle. As you light each candle, moving clockwise from the east, visualize the element of each direction. Make the visualization specific.

As you face east (air), for example, you might breathe deeply and evenly and imagine your intellect as lucid, crystalline, capable of making the necessary decisions. For south (fire), you might imagine you and your lover passionately embracing. When you have finished lighting the candles, stand facing the east and say:

Winds of the east,
Goddess of the feast,
Keep [name of person] with me
So mote it be.

As you face south, say:

Fires of passion
Keep [name] close to me
So mote it be.

As you face west, say:

Waters of our hearts
Never do part
So mote it be.

As you face north, say:

Goddess of the earth
Keep [your name and other person's]
Together for now and ever more.
So mote it be.

Break your Circle. Let the candles burn out naturally, then bury them together in your backyard.

Truth Serum

Perhaps something's fishy and you suspect your lover isn't telling you the truth. This spell lets you see through the smokescreen and get to the heart of the matter. Instead of administering the truth serum to him or her, you drink it yourself to open your second sight. But be sure you really want to know what's going on before you proceed.

Tools:
Water
Nettle
Chamomile
Yarrow
Honey
A cup
A dark blue candle
A candleholder
Matches or a lighter
A scrying tool (a reflective surface such as a dark mirror, a crystal ball, a large clear quartz crystal, or a dark bowl filled with water)
When: On the night of the full moon

Brew an herb tea from the water, nettle, chamomile, and yarrow, and pour it into a cup. Add a little honey to sweeten it. Sip the tea slowly while you allow your mind to relax and grow receptive.

When you've finished the tea, place the candle in its holder and set it on your altar, a table, or other surface so the candle flame will be about at your eye level when you're sitting down. Light the candle and gaze into its flickering flame for a few moments. Set the scrying tool near the candle, so the light reflects in it.

Think about your lover and the issue about which you have concerns. When you feel ready to learn the truth, look into the scrying tool and behold your lover's face before you in the reflective surface. Ask him or her whatever you want to know. You might see visions, hear a verbal response, feel a reaction in your body, or merely sense what's true. Trust your intuition.

Continue scrying for as long as you wish, asking more questions if you desire. When you've received all the information you seek or can process at present, extinguish the candle.

Flirtatious Friend Spell

Is a friend getting a little too friendly with your lover? This spell uses sympathetic magick to convey your message: Hands off!

Tools:
A figurine made of wax, clay, cloth, wood, or another material
A photo of your friend
Clippings of your friend's hair and/or fingernails (optional)
Glue or tape
A marker to write on the figurine
A black ribbon
A box with a lid, big enough to put the figurine in
When: During the waning moon, preferably on a Saturday

If possible, fabricate the figurine (known magickally as a poppet) yourself, but if you aren't handy you can purchase a readymade one. Glue or tape the photo of your friend on the poppet. If you've been able to acquire clippings of your friend's hair and/or fingernails, attach them to the poppet, too.

With the marker write your friend's full name on the poppet. Say aloud:

Figure of [whatever material the poppet is made of],
I name you [your friend's name]
and command you to keep your hands off [your beloved's name].

Tie the poppet's hands with the black ribbon. Place the poppet in the box and close it. Say aloud:

This spell is cast with love and compassion, harming none.
Blessed be.

Put the poppet in the friendship sector of your home. To locate this spot, stand at the door you use most often to enter and leave your home, facing in. The friendship sector is to your right.

A Charm to Safeguard Love
This charm requires all three elements of traditional charms: verbal, written, and physical.

Tools:
Red or purple construction paper (red and purple are the colors of passion and romance)
Rose oil
A picture of you and your mate
Scissors
A pen that writes in red ink
Dab the paper with the rose oil, saying:

Rose of love, this charm's begun,
That I and [name of your partner]
will always be one!

Cut the paper in the shape of a heart. In the middle of the paper put a picture of yourself and your beloved, writing your names underneath, and keep it in a safe place to safeguard that relationship and keep love alive.

Relationship Rescue Pie

If you're lucky enough to have found the right person, you might not need all of these spells to attract a lover or keep him or her faithful. Still, even a really great relationship hits some bumps every once in a while. Whenever your relationship is in need of a pick-me-up, try whipping up an apple pie. Maybe this doesn't sound very spell-like, but remember, Kitchen Witchery can be extremely useful. Besides, apples represent health, cinnamon is a good love herb, vanilla inspires love, and ginger improves overall energy. So bake away!

Tools:
8 medium apples, peeled and thinly sliced
½ teaspoon ginger
½ teaspoon cinnamon
½ teaspoon nutmeg (or to taste)
½ teaspoon vanilla extract
¼ cup flour
2 pie crust sticks, prepared and rolled out according to directions on the box for a 9-inch pie, or from scratch
2 tablespoons butter

Preheat the oven to 425°F. Toss the apple slices with the spices, vanilla, and flour; put them into the bottom of the pie crust. Dot the top of the apples evenly with bits of butter. Put the other half of the pie crust over the top of the pie, securing it at the edges while saying:

Secured within, so my magick begins.
Transform anger with love, and bless from above!

Gently draw a heart in the top of the pie using a fork so that energy bakes into the crust. Bake the pie in the preheated oven for about 45 minutes, or until the crust is brown and apple juice is bubbling through the heart pattern.

A Spell to Clean Up Your Love Life

This spell is based on the feng shui concept that clutter in your home signifies confusion, blockages, and messiness in your life. It requires no tools.

When: Any time—the sooner the better!

Stand at the entrance you use most often to go in and out of your home, facing inside. Locate the furthest, right-hand section of your home (as seen from your doorway). This is your relationship area. Notice what's in this space. If it's cluttered, clean it up. Get rid of old stuff that you don't need or use anymore. In feng shui, old stuff represents old baggage and things from your past that may be holding you back. Organize what you choose to keep so it's neat and orderly.

Pay attention to the things you place in this area, for their symbolism is an important part of the spell. Old, faded, worn-out objects represent a love life that's lost its sparkle. Broken items indicate broken dreams or a physical breakup. Display things in this sector that symbolize what you desire in a romantic relationship or that signify hope, joy, and love.

The Drink of Love

Tools:
The Lovers card from a tarot deck
A glass of spring water
A silver (or silverplate) spoon
A drop of melted honey or a pinch of sugar
When: On a Friday night during the waxing moon

Place the tarot card face up on a windowsill where the moon will shine on it. Set the glass of water on top of the card and leave it overnight. The image of the card will be imprinted into the water. In the morning, use a silver spoon to stir the honey or sugar into the glass to sweeten the water and, symbolically, your relationship. Drink the water with your partner to strengthen the love between you.

Love Talisman

Tools:
A strip of paper
A pen with red ink
A pink or red pouch, preferably made of silk or velvet
2 dried rose petals left from the Spell to Find Your Soulmate
A pinch of cocoa
A pinch of thyme
2 apple seeds
A piece of rose quartz
A small pearl
A purple ribbon
Saltwater
A ritual chalice or cup
When: On the first Friday after the new moon

On the strip of paper, write an affirmation, such as "I now have a lover who's right for me in every way and we are very happy together." Fold the paper three times and slip it into the pouch. Add the rose petals, cocoa, thyme, apple seeds, and gemstones.

Tie the pouch with the ribbon, making six knots. Each time you tie a knot, repeat your affirmation. When you've finished, say, "This is now accomplished in harmony with Divine Will, my own true will, and for the good of all."

Pour the saltwater into your ritual chalice or cup and swirl it around a few times, in a clockwise direction, to energize it. Dip your fingers in the water, and then sprinkle the talisman with the water to charge it. Carry the pouch in your pocket or purse, or place the talisman in the relationship sector of your home (see A Spell to Clean Up Your Love Life in this chapter).

Six is the number of give and take, and it signifies the exchange of energy between two people. Because six is the total of three times two, it represents bringing a wish that involves two people into the three-dimensional realm. When you tie knots, while stating your intention aloud, you fix the energy of your wish permanently into the talisman.

Gemstone Fidelity Spell

The gemstones have two symbolic meanings in this spell. Not only do they represent you and your partner, but also rose quartz is a stone of love and affection, and carnelian represents passion. The ribbon's color—dark blue—indicates strength, sincerity, and permanence; the white cloth offers protection.

Tools:
An obelisk-shaped piece of rose quartz
An obelisk-shaped piece of carnelian
A piece of dark blue ribbon

A piece of white silk
A metal box with a lid, large enough to contain the two gemstones
When: When the moon is in Capricorn

Wash the gemstones with warm, soapy water, and then stand them side by side on your altar so that they are touching. Imagine one embodying your energy, the other your beloved's energy (it doesn't matter which gem you choose to represent which person). Tie the stones together with the ribbon, making two knots, while you envision you and your partner being connected by a strong bond of love and devotion. Cover the gems with the white cloth and leave them until evening.

Once the moon has risen, wrap up the gemstones in the white silk cloth, and then set the package in the box. Take the box outside and bury it in the ground, preferably beneath an oak or apple tree.

Love Bath

Tools:
A tub filled with comfortably hot water
1 teaspoon sea salt
The rest of the rose petals left from the Spell to Find Your Soulmate
A few drops of jasmine, ylang-ylang, patchouli, or rose essential oil
A red or pink candle in a candleholder
Romantic music
When: On a Friday night, during the waxing moon

As you fill your bathtub with water, sprinkle the sea salt into it. Salt acts as both a purifying agent, dispersing any unwanted vibrations, as well as a symbol of the earth element, which is associated with stability, security, and sensuality. Add the essential oil to the bathwater, then scatter the rose petals on top. Light the candle and turn on the music.

Get into the tub and soak pleasantly, as you think loving thoughts about your partner. If you don't yet have a romantic partner, think positive thoughts about the person you intend to attract. If you have a lover, invite him or her to join you in the love bath.

Magick Balm to Heal a Broken Heart

We've all suffered from broken hearts. This spell eases the pain of losing the one you love and helps heal your heart.

Tools:
A small piece of rose quartz
A glass jar or bottle, preferably green, with a lid or stopper
9 ounces olive, almond, or grapeseed oil
6 drops rose, jasmine, or ylang-ylang essential oil
¼ teaspoon dried chamomile leaves
When: Begin on the new moon and continue for as long as necessary

Wash the rose quartz and the jar with mild soap and water. Pour the olive, almond, or grapeseed oil into the jar. Add the essential oil and inhale the fragrance, allowing it to relax your mind. Crush the chamomile leaves very finely and sprinkle them in the oil. Add the rose quartz. Cap the jar and shake it three times to blend and charge the ingredients.

Before going to bed, pour a little of the magick balm into your palm and dip your index finger in it. Then rub the oil on your skin at your heart center. Feel it gently soothing the pain. Take several slow, deep breaths, inhaling the pleasant scent, letting it calm your thoughts and emotions. Repeat each night and each morning until your sadness diminishes.

A Spell to Mend a Romantic Rift

A lovers' quarrel has left you and your partner at odds. Pride, hurt feelings, anger, and other destructive emotions may be preventing you from making up. This spell helps mend the rift between you.

Tools:
A clear quartz crystal
A ballpoint pen
A piece of paper
Jasmine essential oil or Magick Balm (see previous spell)
2 pink candles
Candleholders
Matches or a lighter
When: As soon as possible

Wash the quartz crystal with mild soap and water, then pat it dry. On the piece of paper write down everything you like and enjoy about your partner. When you've finished, put a drop of oil on each corner of the paper and fold it three times. Use the ballpoint pen to inscribe your name on one of the candles and your beloved's name on the other. Dress the candles by rubbing a little oil on them (not on the wicks).

Put the candles in their holders and position them on your altar, a table, or other flat surface, so they are about a foot apart. Lay the folded piece of paper between the candles and set the crystal on top of the paper. Light the candles. Close your eyes and bring to mind an image of your partner. Say to that image:

I honor the divine within you.
I forgive you and I forgive myself.
I am grateful for all the good times we've known together.
I bless you and love you. Namasté.

Let go of all anger, resentment, recrimination, criticism, and so forth that you have held toward your partner. When you're ready, open your eyes and snuff out the candles.

If necessary, repeat the spell the next day, only this time move the two candles a little closer together. Do this spell daily, moving the candles closer each time, until you've mended the rift between you.

Amulet to Block Unwanted Attention

Some people just won't take "no" for answer. If someone seems determined to push his or her way into your life and won't leave you alone, this amulet helps you repel unwanted attention and establish clear boundaries.

Tools:
A black pouch, preferably silk or leather
A piece of amber
A piece of onyx
Pine incense
An incense burner
Matches or a lighter
A piece of paper
A pen with black ink
Dried basil leaves
Anise or fennel seeds
An ash leaf
A white ribbon
Saltwater
When: During the waning moon, preferably on a Saturday

Wash the amber and the onyx with mild soap and water. Fit the incense in its burner and light it.

On the paper, draw a sigil that uses the letters in the word *protection* (see Wiccan Wonderings in Chapter 4). As you work, envision yourself safe and sound, completely surrounded by a sphere of pure white light that no one can penetrate without your permission. When you've finished, draw a circle around the sigil and fold the paper so it's small enough to fit into the pouch.

Put the sigil, botanicals, amber, and onyx into the pouch. Tie it closed with the white ribbon, making eight knots. Each time you tie a knot repeat this incantation aloud:

From energies I don't invite
This charm protects me day and night.

Sprinkle the amulet with saltwater, then hold it in the incense smoke for a few moments to charge it. Wear or carry the amulet with you at all times, until the annoying person stops bothering you.

Chapter 7

Spells for Health

A health spell is no different than any other spell. Its effect is dependent on your intent, your passion and beliefs, and your ability to focus. If you're doing a spell for your own health, you are the one who makes things happen. If you're doing a spell for someone else's health, the effects depend on the other person's willingness to be healed.

Health spells involve many of the same components that other spells do—herbs and incantations, visualizations and affirmations, colors and sounds. They also involve prayer, meditation, and touch. None of these things, however, is a substitute for treatment by a qualified physician or homeopath.

Taking Inventory of Your Health

By taking inventory of your health, you'll have a clearer idea about which spells will work best for you. Spend some time thinking about the following questions:

1. Most of the time, is your energy high or low?
2. When was your last visit to a doctor? Why did you go?
3. Do you have regular checkups?
4. Do you have chronic health problems? If so, what are they?
5. Do you get several colds a year?

6. How much sleep do you need each night?
7. When do you feel happiest and healthiest?
8. Are there certain times of the year when your health is better or worse?
9. Do you worry a lot about your health?
10. Do you worry about death?
11. Do you experience fluctuations in your moods?
12. Do you consider yourself a basically optimistic person?
13. Do you have a particular spiritual belief system?
14. In general, how would you describe your health?
15. Have you noticed any particular patterns to your health?
16. Describe your beliefs about illness and health.
17. Have you ever sought alternative treatments for an illness or disease?
18. Do you meditate?
19. Does anyone in your family or close circle of friends have a chronic illness? If so, what type?
20. Do you consider yourself an open-minded individual?

Pay special attention to your answers to questions concerning your beliefs about health and illness. It may be that the three colds or the flu you get every year is directly related to your belief that getting three colds a year or coming down with the flu during the winter is normal. Read your answers several times. If you find that you hold negative or limiting beliefs concerning health, then changing these beliefs will do more for you than any spell.

The Human Energy Field

"Your body is designed to heal itself," writes Donna Eden in *Energy Medicine*. In fact, we have all the tools we need to heal ourselves, and it begins with an awareness of the subtle energies that give our bodies life. In China, these energies are called *chi* or *qi*. In India and Tibet, the energy is known as *prana*. The Sufis call it *baraka*. It runs through meridians in our bodies and is contained in seven major centers, or chakras, that extend from the base of the spine to the crown of the head.

Chakra literally means a disk or vortex. Imagine a swirling center of energy of various colors and you'll have a pretty good idea of what it looks like. When our energy is balanced, we are healthy. When our energy centers are unbalanced or blocked, we get sick. Each energy center has a particular function and governs certain organs and physical systems within its domain. When a chakra is blocked, unbalanced, or not functioning properly, the organs and systems within its domain suffer the effects.

The energy centers are said to contain everything we have ever felt, thought, and experienced. They are our body's data banks in this life and are imprinted with our soul's history throughout many lives. Illness manifests first in the body's energy field, where it can be seen by an individual who can perceive the field.

When a medical intuitive, for instance, looks at an energy field, he or she is able to perceive a number of details. To a medical intuitive, your chakras make you an open book. You don't have to be a medical intuitive, however, to pick up information about your health or the health of someone else. Sometimes, simply going with your first intuitive impression, going "from the gut," is enough.

Emotional Patterns and the Energy Centers

As you work with your own energy centers through spells, your system will be unique to you. The more you learn about the human energy system, the better equipped you are to maintain your health.

The first energy center is what Caroline Myss, PhD, author of *Sacred Contracts, Anatomy of the Spirit*, and many other books, calls "tribal power." It relates to our families, our framework in life, and where our basic needs are met as children. It's where we learn to trust and to help ourselves. When this center isn't working the way it should, we may experience chronic lower back pain, sciatica, rectal problems, depression, and immune-related disorders.

Energy Centers and Health (Based on Caroline Myss's System)

Chakra	Where	Organs and Systems
1	Base of spine	Immune system, rectum, feet, legs, bones
2	Below navel	Sexual organs, large intestines, appendix, hips, bladder
3	Solar plexus	Abdomen and stomach, upper intestines, liver, kidneys, gallbladder, pancreas, middle vertebrae, adrenal glands
4	Between nipples	Heart and lungs, shoulders and arms, circulatory system, diaphragm, ribs, breasts, thymus gland
5	Throat	Throat, neck, thyroid, parathyroid, trachea, esophagus, mouth, teeth, gums, hypothalamus
6	Middle of forehead	Eyes, ears, nose, brain, nervous system, pineal and pituitary glands
7	Crown	Skeletal system, skin and muscular system

Myss calls the second center "power and relationships." The issues governed by this chakra have to do with individuating ourselves from our tribe—our family. Power issues are invariably involved over our autonomy, money, sex, blame and guilt, and creativity. Money worries often manifest in this area. When this chakra doesn't function correctly, we may have trouble with our reproductive organs, bladder, urinary tract, hips, or pelvis.

The third energy center is what Myss calls "personal power." It is dominant when we're in puberty and are attempting to establish who we are, our "ego self." Issues involved are trust, responsibility for making our own decisions, and our self-esteem. Mona Lisa Schulz, MD, intuitive, and author of *Awakening Intuition*, says this energy center is about "me against the world." When the center is off balance, we have problems such as ulcers, Crohn's disease, anorexia or bulimia, addictions, liver trouble, obesity, and adrenal dysfunction. This center is where many of us experience intuitive insight. A "gut hunch," for example, originates here.

Chakras and Their Corresponding Functions and Colors

Chakra	Color	Function
1	Red	Survival
2	Orange	Sexuality, nurturing
3	Yellow	Emotions, power
4	Green	Compassion, love
5	Blue	Communication
6	Purple	Intuition, intellect
7	White	Spirituality, knowledge

The lower three centers, says Myss, are where most people spend their energy. "Most illnesses result from a loss of energy from these three chakras." Both Myss and Schulz note that even when someone develops a disease related to the upper chakras—heart or neurological problems, for example—the energy origins of the illnesses often come from the bottom three chakras.

The fourth center is known as the heart chakra. It's all about our emotions—how we feel or block them, how we express them, and to whom we express them. It's about identifying what we feel at any given moment. Once we know what we feel, we can take steps to change what needs to be changed in our lives. When this chakra isn't functioning correctly, the physical problems that can result include asthma and allergies, lung cancer, heart attack, bronchial pneumonia, and breast cancer.

The fifth center, the throat chakra, has to do with personal will and expression. This is the area that's engaged in spellwork. It also involves issues such as pursuing and living our dreams, timing, the way we express what we want, and our capacity to make decisions. "Health in this center," writes Schulz, "calls for a balance between expressing ourselves and listening to others; between pushing ourselves forward to fulfill our needs or waiting, when necessary, for things to come to us; and between imposing our will on others or allowing others to impose their will upon us."

When this chakra isn't functioning the way it should, we may experience problems with our throat, gums, and mouth. We may get swollen glands or have thyroid problems. Quite often, the smooth functioning of this chakra depends on expressing what's in our fourth center, in our hearts.

The sixth energy center concerns thought and perception. Its issues concern our intellectual abilities, openness to new ideas, and our ability to learn from experience. When this chakra doesn't function correctly, physical problems such as brain tumors and stroke, or neurological problems such as Parkinson's, seizures, spinal difficulties, and problems with the ears, eyes, and nose, can develop.

The seventh energy center concerns our spirituality and being able to integrate it into our daily lives. It involves finding a sense of our life's purpose. "The failure to connect with our purpose affects us profoundly in the seventh emotional center," Schulz says. In some instances, this failure can prove fatal. After all, if you don't have a reason to live, your body simply shuts down. This energy center is about taking responsibility for creating our own lives.

Some of the physical problems that can occur when this center doesn't function properly are chronic exhaustion, Lou Gehrig's disease, multiple sclerosis, and what Myss calls "energetic disorders."

This is by no means a complete list of emotional patterns related to the various chakras, but it should provide enough information to use the spells in this chapter.

✳ **Wiccan Wonderings: Can you see the human energy field?**
The human energy field extends from a few inches to several feet around the physical body. It's like our personal ozone layer, a buffer. When it's healthy, the colors are brilliant and smooth, but illness and disease may cause it to have dark or white splotches in it, tiny rips or tears or discoloration. With practice, people can train themselves to detect the aura. Some people may see it, others may feel it, and still others may do both.

Essential Oils for Health
Essential oils can be helpful in the health area. Here are some common uses:

1. For warts, try one drop of lemon essential oil applied directly to the wart, daily, until it disappears.
2. When you overindulge, try essential oils of juniper, cedarwood, lavender, carrot, fennel, rosemary, and lemon. Make your own blend of these oils and use a total of six to eight drops in a bath.
3. To relieve depression, make a blend of geranium, lavender, and bergamot in a room diffuser or put six to eight drops in a bath.
4. Rosemary promotes alertness and stimulates memory. Inhale during long car trips or while reading and studying.
5. For restful sleep, put one or two drops of chamomile, lavender, or neroli on your pillow before going to bed.
6. For burns or scalds, apply tea tree oil directly to the affected area.
7. To aid digestion and relieve an upset stomach, put one drop of peppermint oil in half a glass of water and sip slowly.
8. To relieve teething pain in children, use one drop of chamomile oil on a washcloth wrapped around an ice cube.
9. To cool the body in summer and protect it in winter, use one drop of chamomile oil in the bath.
10. When the flu is going around, add a few drops of thyme oil to a diffuser or let it simmer in a pan on the stove.

A Spell to Bolster the First Chakra
For this spell, you're addressing first chakra needs—your "tribe," your ability to provide for life's necessities, your ability to stand up for yourself, and any of the organs and parts of the body that are governed by the first energy center. You can also apply variations of this spell for each of the seven energy centers.

Tools:
Object that represents your "tribe" (a family photo, a photo of
coworkers, a figurine of an animal, something you bought on a
family trip—it doesn't matter, as long as it symbolizes your tribe)
A red candle
Pen and paper
When: Whenever you feel the need

Jot down what you're trying to accomplish. If you're mired in
depression, write an affirmation, such as "I am happy" or "My mood is
great." If you feel insecure within your tribe, then write, "I am safe and
secure" or some other variation on the idea that feels right to you.

Slip the paper under the symbol, light your red candle, and say your
affirmation aloud. Visualize the end result. As always, back it with emotion. Then burn the paper, releasing your desire; let the candle burn
down on its own, and toss it out.

A Spell for a Specific Ailment

First, try to locate the ailment in terms of the energy centers. If the ailment isn't listed in this chapter, then use what you do know. If, for
instance, you have a sinus infection, then you would focus on the sixth
chakra, which governs, among other things, the nose.

Ask yourself questions in terms of the sixth chakra's themes. Are
you closed to new ideas? Are you feeling inadequate?

Once you've decided which chakra or chakras to work with, write
an affirmation that states what you want. For a sinus condition, your
affirmation might be: "I am at peace." Or: "I am well." Light the appropriate colored candle for the chakra you're working on. Focus your full
attention on that chakra and vividly imagine the energy in that area in a
spinning clockwise motion. Do the visualization as long as you can
maintain the energy. Then say the affirmation aloud, burn the piece of
paper on which you wrote it, blow out the candle, and toss it out.

A Spell to Heal an Injury

Green is the color of growth, healthy plants, and comfort—hence the green items used in this spell.

Tools:
A green ribbon
A pen or marker that will write on fabric
A green light bulb
When: As needed

On the ribbon, write an affirmation, making sure to state the end result you desire. For instance, say, "My arm is whole and healthy." Then tie the ribbon loosely near the injured body part (but not directly over the wound).

Screw the green light bulb into a lamp or fixture. Position yourself so the green light shines on the injured body part. Visualize the injury being completely healed. If you have a broken bone, see the pieces knitting together again perfectly. Imagine a cut mending and the skin healing without a scar. Envision swelling and bruises fading away. Make sure to focus on the end result you desire, not the injury, and repeat your affirmation frequently.

Shine the light on the injury several times per day. Leave the ribbon in place until the injury is healed.

Create a Strength and Safety Amulet

The idea for this amulet comes from India.

Tools:
Piece of tree bark (see directions)
Yellow or gold yarn
White cloth

To make the amulet, go out at dawn and pluck a small piece of bark from the east side of a tree (where it gets the morning light). Bind this with the yarn, saying:

Gathered from where the sun awoke,
The power of protection and strength I invoke!

Wrap the bark in a natural white cloth (so it won't get damaged) and carry it with you often.

A Spell to Relieve Digestive Complaints

Tools:
A glass cup
Chamomile tea
A piece of paper
A pen with green ink
Tape
When: Any time

On the paper, write the words *balance, harmony, peace, love,* and *acceptance.* Tape the paper to a clear glass cup, so the words face in. Then brew some chamomile tea and pour it into the glass cup. Let the tea sit for a few minutes to allow the words to imprint their message into the liquid.

Sip the tea slowly, focusing on its soothing warmth in your stomach. Envision healing green light entering your stomach and abdomen, calming the upsets in your digestive tract. Feel yourself relaxing and becoming more receptive to nourishment. Repeat this ritual daily, until your problem improves.

A Spell to Get Rid of a Headache

Tools:
A smoky quartz crystal
A piece of rose quartz
Lavender-scented incense
When: Any time

Wash the stones in running water, then charge them by letting them sit in the sunlight for several minutes. Light the incense. Sit quietly in a comfortable spot and begin breathing slowly and deeply. Hold the rose quartz in your left hand and feel it gently emitting loving, peaceful vibrations. Hold the smoky quartz crystal to your forehead and imagine the quartz absorbing the pain. When you're finished, cleanse and charge the stones again.

A Spell to Quell the Common Cold

If it's cold and flu season, and you're feeling under the weather, a little herbal magick plus some TLC can relieve those miserable symptoms fast and make you feel better all over.

Tools:
Spring water
Hyssop leaves and flowers
An aqua beeswax candle with a cotton wick
A candleholder
Matches or a lighter
When: As needed

Brew a strong tea from the hyssop leaves and/or flowers. Strain the herb residue from the water. Fill a bathtub with comfortably hot water and add the tea to it. Fit the candle in its holder and light it. Get into the tub and soak for as long as you like, inhaling the soothing scent of hyssop.

Focus your mind on loving thoughts and feelings. Envision yourself surrounded by love. As you inhale, imagine you are bringing love into your body. See and sense love circulating through your entire body, from head to foot. Spend several minutes doing this. Let the loving energy gently nourish you, strengthening your system so it can throw off the cold.

Remain in the tub for as long as you like. After you get out of the bathwater, extinguish the candle. Repeat this ritual whenever you like.

Weight Loss Potion

Other than the usual diet-and-exercise regime, is there anything you can do to shed those unwanted pounds? This magick potion works at a subconscious level to silence hunger pangs.

Tools:
Spring water
Unsweetened green apple tea (not spiced apple)
A hot pink ceramic cup
A hot pink candle
A candleholder
Matches or a lighter
When: During the waning moon

When you feel hungry, instead of eating something you shouldn't, brew a pot of green apple tea. Pour the tea into the bright pink cup. Fit the candle into its holder, set it on the dining room or kitchen table, and light it. Sit and gaze at the candle while you inhale the refreshing scent of the tea. Drink the cup of tea slowly, keeping your attention focused on the candle. Feel your hunger pangs gradually subside. Repeat as necessary.

Ritual to Increase Vitality

Tools:
4 bayberry candles
4 clear quartz crystals
When: As needed

Perform this ritual outside. Place the candles at the four compass directions. Set the crystals between the candles to form a Circle. Step inside the Circle and light the candles, beginning in the east and working in a clockwise direction. Stand facing east, with your arms outstretched at your sides, parallel to the ground, palms up.

The candles represent the fire element and the masculine force. The crystals symbolize the earth element and the feminine force. Feel the balanced energy around you flowing into your body from every direction. Receive it in your open hands and allow it to fill you up, energizing you.

Draw Mother Earth's nurturing energy upward through your feet, into your legs, torso, arms, and head. Feel the sun's vitalizing energy flowing into the top of your head and down through your body, all the way to your feet. Envision the two forces—yin and yang, heaven and earth—blending and balancing one another in your heart center.

Stand in the center of the Circle as long as you choose. When you feel invigorated, extinguish the candles in a counterclockwise direction and leave the Circle. Repeat this ritual as often as needed. If you wish, you can invite other people to join you in the healing Circle.

Stress-Buster Ritual

Stress is endemic in Western culture. You may not be able to avoid stress, but you can keep it from getting you down. This ritual helps you release stress and stay calm in the presence of everyday annoyances.

Tools:
Soothing music (New Age or classical is best, either instrumental or chanting, without a catchy rhythm or lyrics)
A tumbled chunk of amethyst
A tumbled chunk of rose quartz
A blue candle
A candleholder
A ballpoint pen
Essential oil of lavender, vanilla, sweet orange, or ylang-ylang
Matches or a lighter
When: Any time

Wash the stones with mild soap and water, then pat them dry. Start the music you've chosen. Cast a Circle around the area where you will do your spell. With the ballpoint pen inscribe the word *peace* on the candle. Dress the candle by rubbing it with essential oil (not on the wick). Fit the candle in its holder and light it.

Hold one gemstone in each hand. Sit in a comfortable place and close your eyes. Begin breathing slowly and deeply. Inhale the soothing scent and allow it to calm your mind. Rub the smooth stones with your fingers. Feel the stones neutralize stress, irritability, and anxiety. Focus on your breathing, paying attention to each inhalation and exhalation. If your mind starts to wander, gently bring it back and say or think the word *peace.*

Spend at least ten minutes this way, longer if you wish. When you feel ready, open your eyes and extinguish the candle. Let the music continue playing or shut it off. Carry the stones with you and rub them whenever stress starts to mount.

A Spell for Maintaining Health

Take an old knitted glove that you've worn and stuff it with healthful dry herbs (symbolically, you are stuffing yourself with all that positive energy). Some good options include caraway, coriander, fern, geranium petals, juniper, marjoram, nutmeg, tansy, and thyme. When you're done, sew up the opening (so the health remains where you put it), tie a strand of your hair around the pointer finger of the glove (to remind you of good health and its blessings), and keep it with your clothing.

Strength and Safety Soup

Here's a recipe to use during those times when you feel you need more protection. Garlic and onions are the key ingredients. Romans used garlic for strength, and many other people have considered it a protective herb. Egyptians used onions to keep away baleful spirits and fed them to their slaves to ensure vitality. This recipe also relies on the number four for its earthy energy, which provides the magick with foundations to take root in our hearts and lives.

Tools:
1 large Spanish onion
1 large red onion
1 bundle green onions
1 white onion
1 tablespoon butter
4 small cloves garlic, peeled and crushed
4 stalks celery, diced (optional)
2 cups beef stock
2 cups chicken stock
2 cups water
4 dashes Worcestershire sauce (or to taste)
Garlic powder and onion power (optional)
Croutons and grated cheese (for garnish, optional)

Slice the onions and place them in a frying pan with the butter and garlic. For a heartier broth, add the diced celery (to be fried with the onions). Magickally, this ingredient will provide you with psychic insight and a sense of inner peace. Gently sauté the onions, garlic, and celery, if desired, until golden brown.

Stir the vegetables counterclockwise as they cook to banish negative energies, saying:

> *Onions for health, and to keep ghosts at bay,*
> *Garlic for safety all through the day!*

Keep repeating the incantation slowly until the onions are done.

Transfer the onions into a large soup pan, adding the stock, water, and Worcestershire sauce (you might also add a bit of garlic powder and onion powder, but that's optional). Cook this mixture down over a medium-low flame until it is reduced by 2 cups.

Serve the soup with croutons and fresh grated cheese, if desired. Visualize your body being filled with white light as you eat it.

Casting a Health Spell for Another Person

Tools:
Something that represents the other person (a photo or object the person has given you)
Sprig of sage
Eucalyptus oil
A gold candle
A purple or violet candle
When: As needed

Set the object in the middle of your work area or altar, with a candle on either side of it, and the oil burner behind it.

Smudge your work area first and also smudge the object that represents the other person. Pour several drops of eucalyptus oil into your burner. Light it, then light the candles. After a moment of reflection in which you fix the person's face and being in your mind, say:

As the oil and candles burn,
Illness gone and health return,
For my [state relationship and name]
Who is yearning,
And so deserving.

Blow out the candle in the oil burner. Let the other two candles burn down naturally, then toss them out.

※ **Wiccan Wonderings: What needs to be considered before casting a spell for another person's health?**

First, always ask that person's permission. It may be that the illness or disease the person has serves some function in his or her life. The individual may not see it this way, but on some level, it may be true. Even when you do get permission, stick to a general spell to bolster the individual's overall physical health rather than work on any specific area or complaint.

A Spell to Boost Your Energy

Sometimes, we just feel depleted. We need a day off from work simply to laze around and read, go swimming, or take a long walk in the country-side. We aren't sick, we aren't recovering from any illness—we just need to refuel ourselves. For those times, this is the spell you need.

Tools:
Your favorite music
Rose quartz
Vervain
When: As needed

This spell is best done when you're alone because you're going to crank up the music. Select music that boosts your spirits and makes you want to move around and dance. The rose quartz is intended to amplify the surge in your mood. The vervain, when burned, provides a general boost to the spirit and cleanses negative vibes, among other things.

Light the vervain, put the quartz next to it, then put on your music and turn the volume up. Let the music suffuse the room and permeate your senses. Then get up and dance to it. Continue as long as needed.

Chapter 8

Spells for Luck, Prosperity, and Abundance

Ask any of your family, friends, and acquaintances what prosperity and abundance mean to them, and the responses are sure to span a broad spectrum. Answers might range anywhere from having enough or more money, being rich, or being in a better job; to having a strong, loving marriage or significant relationship; to writing a bestselling novel. Whether it's owning a horse or owning a home, the answers are always different. Most people yearn for prosperity and abundance, yet these concepts are rather abstract.

What about your own personal view? Do you define prosperity in terms of financial security? Or is your idea of prosperity more about having good health and happiness? Does abundance mean having more of everything or having enough of everything? These distinctions may seem unimportant, but before you work with spells involving prosperity and abundance, it's wise to recognize what these concepts mean to you.

Defining Your Concept of Prosperity and Abundance

Our lives are in a constant state of flux. Once that horse is owned, that novel hits the bestseller lists, or that ideal relationship is found, our ideas about prosperity and abundance change accordingly. Think about what prosperity and abundance mean to you today, right now, in this moment. Finish the phrases below with your true feelings, but don't think too hard about them. The idea is to bypass your rational left brain and allow your intuitive right brain to express itself.

1. I am happiest when . . .
2. My wildest dream is to . . .
3. Given the choice, I would most like to spend my time . . .
4. I thoroughly enjoy . . .
5. I would love to . . .
6. I now spend my free time . . .
7. I feel a sense of accomplishment when . . .
8. My greatest passion is . . .
9. One of my favorite hobbies is . . .

In this exercise, you identified things that make you feel happy and prosperous. Now find an object that represents each entry on your list. Select these objects with care; they're going on your altar and will be used in spells.

Let's say that your wildest dream is to get your pilot's license. Any number of objects might be selected to represent that dream: a model airplane, a photograph of the type of plane you would like to fly, even a child's plastic toy plane. The point is to choose something that immediately connects you to the feeling. Once you've selected your symbolic objects, you're ready to prepare your altar.

Be Careful What You Wish For

At some point in your spellcasting, something will drive home the truth of the old adage, "Be careful what you wish for. You may just get it." This adage speaks to the power of intent. If you ask for abundance or financial freedom, consider your wish carefully. How will that abundance or financial freedom affect your family? Your relationship with your friends? Your job and living situation? Unforeseen repercussions have a way of creeping up, so think things through!

The Color of Money

In terms of spells, the color of money is green. In other words, if you don't have prosperity consciousness—the belief that you are deserving—then you need to develop it before you attempt a spell for prosperity.

Louise Hay, writing in *You Can Heal Your Life*, devotes a chapter to prosperity. She provides a list of negative money beliefs and then illustrates how you can change any of the beliefs you may hold. For prosperity, she writes, it's necessary to:

- Feel deserving
- Make room for the new
- Be happy for other people's prosperity
- Be grateful

To these, she adds, "Love your bills."

"What?!" you're probably saying. "My credit card bills? My electric bill? My mortgage payment? This woman's crazy." But the more you think about it, the less you'll balk. After all, a bill is simply an acknowledgment that a company trusts that you can and will pay—a sort of cosmic honor system. Why should you resent it? Money and prosperity are expressions of living in a universe that is infinitely abundant. All of us can tap into that abundance without depriving someone else. It simply boils down to belief.

While you're building your new belief in prosperity, make symbolic gestures. Drop your loose change into the Salvation Army pot at Christmas. Buy yourself something special. Treat yourself to dinner at your favorite restaurant. Buy a hardback book that you really want. Create your own affirmation about prosperity—and always phrase it in the present tense. Write or say it at least a dozen times a day for as long as it takes for your unconscious to get the message. Be sure to back that affirmation with emotion.

And post this quotation from Louise Hay's book in a spot where you'll see it frequently: "True prosperity begins with feeling good about yourself . . . it is never an amount of money; it is a state of mind. Prosperity or lack of it is an outer expression of the ideas in your head."

A Spell to Create New Beliefs

Tools:
14 green scented candles
An empty glass container
When: On the new moon

While you're still in the process of writing your affirmation, buy fourteen scented green candles. Small candles are good for this, the kind that are sold for aromatherapy burners. On the night of the next new moon, light one of the candles at your altar or special place. While it's burning, say your affirmation aloud and feel its truth. After five minutes, blow the candle out and rub your hands in the smoke. Wave the smoke toward your face, your body, your clothes. Remember that fragrance, associate it with abundance, prosperity, and your new belief. Set the candle aside where you can see it.

✳ **Wiccan Wonderings: What's the most important ingredient in any spell?**
It always boils down to belief. Remember, Dorothy got back to Kansas because she trusted the wizard when he told her all she had to do was close her eyes and click her heels three times. It worked because she believed in magick.

Repeat this for the next fourteen days, using a new candle each time, until the next full moon. Set each spent candle next to its predecessor. On the night of the full moon, after you have burned the fourteenth candle, light all fourteen and let them burn down. Then pour the wax into a glass container.

This candle symbolizes your new belief about prosperity. Once the wax has solidified, toss it out, thus sending that belief out into the universe. Each time you do this spell, remember to give thanks.

A Spell to Fulfill Your Desire

Tools:
A green scented candle
An object that represents your desire (choose from your list)
When: During the waxing moon

At night, under the waxing phase of the moon, light a green candle at your special place. State your need or intention. Place or focus on something on your altar that represents this need or intention and repeat your affirmation. Visualize the manifestation of whatever it is you need. Don't worry about how it will manifest; simply trust that your wish will be fulfilled. Blow out the candle and leave it and your symbolic objects on the altar. Be grateful for all that you do have.

Repeat as often as you feel is necessary during the waxing moon. When you trust that what you need is forthcoming (and yes, this does take trust), clear your altar and let the candle burn all the way down. Then toss it out and release it.

Gotta Have It Spell

Whether you've got your eye on a pair of designer shoes, a brand-new gadget, or a sports car, this spell helps you obtain whatever your heart desires. You can magickally manifest big things as easily as little ones. The only limits are in your own mind.

Tools:
A clear quartz crystal or an "abundance" crystal (one that contains a greenish mineral called chlorite)
A picture or other likeness of the object you've "gotta have"
Essential oil of cedar
When: During the waxing moon, preferably on a Thursday

Wash the crystal in mild soap and water. Hold the crystal in your left hand while you gaze at the picture of the item you've "gotta have" and imagine yourself already owning it. Involve your feelings and senses in the visualization—the more vivid you can make the experience, the better.

When your mind starts to drift, dab four dots of essential oil on the picture, one at each corner. Let the scent reinforce your intention to acquire the object you desire. When you feel confident that you'll receive your heart's desire, open the Circle you created to conduct the spell. Place the picture on your altar, desk, or another place where you'll see it often. Set the crystal on top of the picture to increase the power of your spell. Look at the picture regularly, reaffirming your intention, until the object materializes.

Go Fly a Kite

What do you wish for? A new car? A better job? Money to take a dream vacation? The sky's the limit! This high-flying spell sends your requests far and wide so the universe can fulfill your heart's desires.

Tools:
A kite
Ribbons of different colors
A pen that will write on fabric
When: Depends on your intentions

Collect the ingredients needed for this spell. Select ribbons of colors that correspond to your desires: pink for love, gold for money, and so on. On each ribbon, write one wish. Remember to state your request in the form of an affirmation. Attach the ribbons to a kite. Visualize your wishes coming true.

Take the kite outside to an open area where you can fly it without interference. As you watch the kite soaring in the sky, imagine the wind catching your requests and carrying them to the four corners of the earth. Have fun—a positive attitude will help your intentions manifest faster.

A Spell to Increase Your Income

The color green is obviously important in money spells. White, however, can also be useful because it represents understanding.

Tools:
Green and white candles
A deck of tarot cards
An object that represents your desire (consult your list again!)
A pen with green ink and a piece of paper
When: During the waxing moon

Put your candles at opposite ends of your altar. Between them, place an object that represents your desire to increase your income. This can be an object that symbolizes something on your list or anything else—a coin, a dollar bill, a sacred stone, whatever you want.

From your deck of tarot cards, remove the suit of pentacles, which represents money, the Star, and the nine of cups. In front of the white candle, place the ace of pentacles; it symbolizes new financial undertakings and opportunities. In front of the green candle, put the ten of pentacles; it's called the "Wall Street" card and symbolizes a financial windfall. In the middle of the two candles, place the nine of cups—the wish card—and the Star, which symbolizes, among other things, success.

Now light the candles and say:

The money I spend
or the money I lend
comes back to me
in multiples of three.

Visualize the figure you have in mind. Jot it down on the piece of paper. Imagine what you can do with an increase in your income. The more vivid you can make your visualization, backed with intense emotion, the faster it will manifest. This ritual can be as short or as long as you want. The point is to do it with full conscious awareness and intent, backed with emotion. End the spell by blowing out the candle and giving thanks, then toss away the candle.

On the next night, repeat the ritual, but with certain changes. First, remove the two and five of pentacles from your deck. You don't want these two cards on your altar. The two of pentacles means you're robbing Peter to pay Paul; the five means poverty and heavy debt.

Light your candles. Say the poem. Then take the remaining cards and place them between the ace and ten of pentacles, the nine of cups (the wish card), and the Star. Visualize, affirm, then blow out the candles and throw them away. Keep everything else on the altar as it is overnight.

> ✳ **Wiccan Wonderings: What can you do when money seems to be going out faster than it's coming in?**
> Here's a quick fix: Buy a roll of purple, violet, or lavender ribbon—the kind you find in the gift wrap area of most drug stores and supermarkets. Tie a piece of ribbon around every faucet in your home, and as you do so, say: "As water flows, my finances grow."

On the third night, light the candles and give thanks for everything you have; repeat the poem and feel the reality of your increase in income taking form around you. Blow out the candles and toss them away.

Keep saying the poem as long as you need to, as often as you like, even after the increase begins to manifest.

A Spell to Say Goodbye to Debt

Remember that even quick-and-easy spells must be done with vivid intent and visualization. In terms of tools for this one, you can substitute something for the five of pentacles that represents your debt, but make sure it will burn.

Tools:
A red candle
Tarot's five of pentacles
Empty bowl
When: During the waning moon

Light the red candle. Red represents energy and what you're doing here is drawing on energy to cancel your debt. Say the following words:

Debt begone
lickety split,
debt begone
before I spit.

Then take the five of pentacles or whatever object symbolizes your debt and pass it through the candle flames until it catches fire. Let it burn to ashes in the empty bowl. Pinch out the candle's flame, then toss out the candle. On the next new moon, bury the ashes far from your home.

A Spell to Create Prosperity

This spell can be used for any kind of prosperity, but it works best for the prosperity of inner peace, the source of all true prosperity. Sage is a good herb for getting rid of negativity and cinnamon is excellent for boosting your energy and creativity.

Tools:
Sprig of sage
A green candle
Empty bowl
Pinch of cinnamon

When: During the new moon

On the night of the new moon, put the green candle in the empty bowl with the sage. Light them both. As you sprinkle cinnamon into the flame, say: "I embrace prosperity and inner peace."

Repeat these words and keep sprinkling cinnamon into the flame until the cinnamon is gone. Let the candle and the sage burn down, then bury them in your garden or yard. If you do this during the winter, you can bury the remains in the dirt of an indoor plant.

An Oil to Attract Money
This oil works for attracting things other than money, too.

Tools:
1 pint mineral oil
A clear quart bottle
7 lodestones (found in most New Age bookstores)
A pinch or two of iron filings
Small dark glass bottles
Labels and a pen with green ink

Pour the mineral oil into the bottle, add the lodestones and iron filings, then charge your concoction in the sunlight, preferably when the sun is rising, for seven days. Transfer your oil to smaller bottles with dark glass, label them, and put them in the dark. To bring in money, rub some oil on your thumb and forefinger, then rub your fingertips on money before you spend it. The idea is that the charged, magnetic oil will attract money into your life.

Prosperity Oil
This versatile magick potion has many applications and can be used alone or in conjunction with other spells. Dress candles with it. Dab it on talismans or sigils. Anoint gemstones, crystals, or magick tools with

it. Rub a little on your body. However you use it, this prosperity oil helps you attract all forms of abundance.

Tools:
A green glass bottle with a lid or stopper
A small piece of tiger's eye or aventurine
4 ounces olive, almond, or grapeseed oil
A few drops of peppermint essential oil
Gold or silver glitter
When: During the waxing moon, preferably on a Thursday

Wash the bottle and gemstone with mild soap and water, then dry them. Pour the olive, almond, or grapeseed oil into the bottle. Add the peppermint essential oil and glitter. Drop the tiger's eye or aventurine into the mixture, then put the lid or stopper on the bottle and shake three times to charge the potion.

Apply your Prosperity Oil in whatever manner you choose. You can rub it directly on your body, dress candles with it, dab it on crystals and gemstones, or use it to anoint talismans. In fact, this magick oil can be incorporated into most of the spells in this chapter.

A Spell to Attract Financial Opportunities
Before you do this spell, read the section in Chapter 2 on the correspondences between astrological planets and days of the week. Also glance through Chapter 3 to refresh your memory about the importance of the cardinal points in casting spells.

Tools:
A gold candle
Your favorite scented oil
Clear quartz crystal
Pen and paper
When: On a Thursday during the new moon

Thursday is Jupiter's day, the planet in astrology that represents expansion, and expansion is what you're attempting to do with this spell. Place the gold candle at the northern end of your altar, the direction that represents, among other things, fertility. On the piece of paper, write: I embrace all opportunities for expanding my financial base. Place the piece of paper in front of the candle and put the quartz crystal on top of it. The crystal acts as a magnifier of your thoughts.

Light the candle, and visualize new financial opportunities flowing into your life. Read aloud what you have written down. Then burn the paper, releasing the desire. Let the candle burn down and toss it out. As always, give thanks for the prosperity you already have.

A Quick Spell for Prosperity

One of the most frequent complaints people have about casting spells is that they take so much time. So here's a sixty-second spell to increase your general prosperity.

Tools:
Any purple, violet, or lavender object
Piece of paper and a pen
When: Whenever you feel the need, but most powerful on the
new moon

Jot down the specific things you're trying to create in terms of prosperity. Tuck the list under the purple object, and make it so.

A Spell to Deflect Negative Energy

Take any reflective surface (pieces of aluminum foil or small mirrors, for example), and put them under the light of a midday sun (symbolically this turns away all darkness), saying:

Negativity away,
Darkness away,

Banished by the light of day!

Put these items in every window of your home, and make sure each one is facing outward.

A Spell to Attract Luck

Tools:
A coin minted in the year of your birth
A cabbage leaf
Ribbon or string
Natural fiber cloth

If you can, use a coin with high silver or gold content. Wrap the coin in the cabbage leaf (a good-luck food), and tie the bundle with the ribbon or string to bind the energy (choose the color of the string to correspond with your "lucky" or power color). Leave the cabbage leaf where it will naturally dry without molding (preferably during a waxing moon cycle so that luck "grows"). When it is completely dry, wrap it in the cloth and carry it with you regularly.

Buried Treasure Spell

Instead of hunting for that hidden pirate's chest of gold doubloons, in this spell you symbolically stash treasure in order to "prime the pump" so greater riches can flow to you.

Tools:
9 coins (any denomination)
A small mirror
A tin box with a lid
A magnet
A shovel
When: During the waxing moon, preferably on a Thursday

Place the mirror in the bottom of the tin box, with the reflective side up. Lay the coins, one at a time, on top of the mirror while you envision each one multiplying exponentially. Attach the magnet to the inside of the box (on the lid or a side) and visualize it attracting a multitude of coins to you. Put the lid on the box.

Take your "treasure chest" and the shovel outside and dig a hole beneath a large tree. Bury the box in the ground near the tree's roots. When you've finished, say this incantation aloud:

By the luck of three times three
This spell now brings great wealth to me.
The magnet draws prosperity.
The mirror doubles all it sees.
My fortune grows as does this tree
And I shall ever blessed be.

Money Tree Spell

Money may not grow on trees, but you can tap the growth symbolism inherent in trees with this spell to increase your income.

Tools:
Gold and/or silver ribbons
Small charms, earrings, beads, crystals
Bells or wind chimes
When: During the waxing moon, preferably in the spring or summer; in the fall or winter, do the spell when the waxing moon is in Taurus

Tie the ribbons loosely on the branches of a favorite tree that's special to you. Hang the other adornments on the branches as well. These objects represent gifts or offerings to the nature spirits, in return for their assistance in bringing you wealth. As you attach each item, state your intention aloud and ask the nature spirits to help you acquire what you desire. When you've finished, thank the tree and the nature spirits.

Elemental Money Spell

You've heard of leprechauns, who are said to possess pots of gold. These mythical characters are based on the earth elementals known as gnomes. If you're nice to them, they'll help you acquire your own pot of gold.

> *Tools:*
> Chocolate mint cookies
> A cauldron or bowl
> *When:* During the waxing moon, preferably when the sun and/or moon is in Taurus

Bake or buy chocolate mint cookies. Put a few cookies in your cauldron or bowl and take them outside to a place in nature. Set the cauldron under a bush or at the foot of a tree. Call to the gnomes and tell them you've brought them a gift. Explain that you need money and you know they can help you acquire the wealth you desire. Ask for their assistance and thank them in advance for helping you. Treat them with respect, just as you would a person whose aid you were soliciting.

In a day or so, return to the spot with more cookies. Put the cookies in the cauldron or bowl and call to the gnomes again. Do the same thing a day or so later. Soon you may notice money, valuables, or financial opportunities coming into your life, perhaps in unexpected ways. Repeat the spell as needed to keep the flow of wealth coming your way.

A Spell to Become a Millionaire

You probably don't believe you can become a millionaire, do you? And that's why you haven't already amassed your million dollars. This spell starts reprogramming your subconscious to believe you can attract a cool million—and more importantly, to believe that you deserve it.

Tools:
A likeness of a $1,000,000 bill
A clear quartz crystal or an "abundance" crystal (one that contains a greenish mineral called chlorite)
When: During the waxing moon

Find a likeness of a $1,000,000 bill. You may be able to download an image from the Internet. Or, simply cut a piece of paper the size and shape of a bill, then write One Million Dollars on it. If you wish, add other images to make the bill look as realistic as possible.

Place the million-dollar bill face up on your desk, your altar, or in the wealth sector of your home. (To locate this, stand at the entrance to your home—the one you use most often, not necessarily the front door—with your back to the door, so you're looking inside. The left-hand rear corner is the wealth sector.) Wash the crystal with mild soap and water, then set it on top of the bill. Several times each day, pick up the bill and stare at it as you recite the following affirmation:

I now have $1,000,000 free and clear, to do with as I please.
This money comes to me in harmony with Divine Will, my own true will, and for the good of all, harming none.
I deserve this money and I accept it thankfully.

You don't have to know how the money will come to you, all you have to do is believe it is already on its way. Repeat this spell until you succeed.

Mint Your Own

Wouldn't it be nice if you could mint your own money? Well, now you can. No, we're not talking about counterfeiting. Instead, use magick to make your wealth grow.

Tools:
A likeness of a $1,000,000 bill
A green ceramic flowerpot
Potting soil
Spearmint or peppermint seeds, or a small mint plant
Water
When: During the waxing moon, preferably when the sun or moon is
in Taurus

Make a second $1,000,000 bill, like the one you used in the previous
spell. Gather all the ingredients listed above. Fold the bill three times
and place it in the bottom of the ceramic flowerpot. Fill the pot with
soil. Plant the seeds or seedling in the soil and water it. As you work,
repeat this incantation:

Every day
In every way
Prosperity
Now comes to me.

Set the flowerpot in a spot where light and other conditions are
favorable. Continue caring for your mint plant and remember to recite
the incantation daily. When you trim the plant, save the leaves and dry
them to use in talismans. As the plant grows, so will your finances.

Feng Shui Wealth Spell
In feng shui, red and purple are considered lucky colors. Plants symbolize growth.

Tools:
A plant with red or purple flowers
When: During the waxing moon

Stand at the door you use most often when going in and out of your home, facing inside. Locate the farthest left-hand corner of your home, from this vantage point. That's your wealth sector. Put the plant in that area to make your wealth grow.

Water, feed, and care for the plant with loving kindness. As you tend it and watch it grow, you'll notice your fortune improves.

Prosperity Brew

Tools:
Fresh or dried parsley
Fresh or dried mint leaves
1 cup water
Pot
Wooden spoon
Strainer
When: During the new moon

On the night of the new moon, pour a cup of water into a pot and begin heating it on the stove. Put the parsley and mint in the water and say, "I embrace prosperity and open myself to receive abundance of all kinds." Stir the brew with a wooden spoon, making three clockwise circles to charge the mixture. Bring the water to a boil, then turn off the stove and allow the brew to cool. Strain the water, then pour it on the plant you placed in your wealth sector in the previous spell or use it to water other plants in your home or yard.

A Mail Spell for Prosperity
This spell is based on the threefold law.

Tools:
A $5 bill
Yellow construction paper

Take the money and wrap it the construction paper, saying:

Return to me
By the law of three.

Mail this off anonymously to someone you know who is in need of a little extra cash. This spell usually yields a $15 return within three weeks.

A Money Talisman

Tools:
A strip of paper
A pen with green, gold, or silver ink
Peppermint essential oil
A green pouch (preferably made of silk or velvet)
A coin (any denomination)
3 whole cloves
A pinch of cinnamon
A gold or silver ribbon 9 inches long
Cedar chips
Pine or sandalwood incense
When: During the waxing moon

On the strip of paper, write an affirmation, such as "I now have plenty of money for everything I need and desire. Riches come to me from all directions."

Dot the corners of the paper with essential oil, then fold it three times and slip it into the pouch. Add the coin, cedar, and herbs to the pouch. Tie the pouch with the ribbon, making three knots. Each time you tie a knot, repeat your affirmation. When you've finished, say, "This is now accomplished in harmony with Divine Will, my own true will, and with good to all." Light the incense, and hold the talisman in the incense smoke to charge it. Carry the pouch in your pocket or purse. If you prefer, use the talisman in your place of business. You can put it in your safe, cash register, or money drawer.

Crystal Abundance Spell

Some quartz crystals contain bits of greenish mineral matter in them. These are known as "money crystals." If possible, acquire one of these to use in this spell. The amplifying energy of the crystal combined with the symbolism of the color green can enhance your spell.

Tools:
A quartz crystal
An image that represents abundance
When: On a Thursday when the moon is waxing

Select a magazine picture that symbolizes prosperity to you. Or choose an image of an object or condition you desire—a new home, a sports car, a European vacation—and set it face up on a windowsill where the moon's light will shine on it.

Wash the crystal in warm water with mild soap to cleanse it of any ambient energies. Dry the crystal, then hold it to your third eye while thinking about your intention; this projects the image into the crystal. Then set the crystal on the picture. Make sure the crystal's point faces toward the inside of your home, to draw abundance from the universe to you. Leave the crystal in place overnight. In the morning, remove the crystal and picture and give thanks for the bounty you are about to receive.

A Fetish to Fight Bad Luck

We've all run into streaks of bad luck. Whip up a few of these fetishes, and you'll neatly disperse that negative energy.

Tools:
3 pennies

3 pieces of loosely woven cloth (in your lucky color)
3 pieces of white string

Use the string to tie each of the pennies into the cloth while reciting an incantation:

In luck I trust, in luck I believe,
Within this bundle, protection weave!

When you want to activate the fetish, take it to a remote location and put it into the earth, saying:

Bad fortune's come, but not to stay.
I command it now to turn away.

Turn away from the bundle and don't look back, leaving all that negative energy behind you.

✳ **Wiccan Wonderings: When doing spells for prosperity, does it take away someone else's prosperity?**
Not at all. Prosperity and abundance don't have limits. You may have trouble, however, if you're casting spells to win the lottery or at gambling, or if you're attempting to swindle someone out of money.

Affirmations for Prosperity

The power of affirmations can't be emphasized too strongly, particularly in the area of prosperity and abundance. Even if you don't believe in the power of words, if you say something enough times, your unconscious mind begins to believe it and your reality begins to shift.

It can work for things both simple and grand. Are you waiting for a check that hasn't arrived? Then fifty times a day, repeat, "My check is here," or "My check arrives." Or perhaps you need extra money this month for renovations on your home. In this instance, you might say, "I have enough money to do the renovations."

Try not to concern yourself with how you're going to get that extra money. Simply be aware that opportunities will begin to present themselves to you if you continue to say the affirmation. Be alert for patterns of coincidence, which can serve as signposts to new opportunities. And always phrase your affirmation in the present tense!

Keep It Coming Prosperity Circle

Even if your present financial situation is sound, you can't predict what the future may bring. This spell ensures that you'll always have more than enough money to cover your expenses.

Tools:
9 small jars (baby food jars are perfect)
Coins (any denomination)
A piece of paper
A pen that writes green, gold, or silver ink
When: Daily, beginning during the waxing moon

Choose a spot in your home or workplace where you can leave the jars in position permanently, where they won't be disturbed. Arrange the empty jars in a circle. On the paper, write the following affirmation:

I now have plenty of money for everything I need and desire and plenty to share with others.

Lay the paper in the center of the circle of jars and put a coin on top to secure it. Then, beginning at the east, work in a clockwise direction and drop one coin in each jar. Repeat the affirmation aloud each time you place a coin in a jar.

The next day add another coin to each jar, again starting at the east and working in a clockwise direction. Continue in this manner, adding one coin per day to each jar. When all the jars are full, remove the coins and donate the money to your favorite charity.

As you give the money away, repeat the following affirmation three times:

I offer this money with love and gratitude.
I now receive my tenfold return, with good to all concerned.

Start filling the jars again, in the same manner as before. Continue performing this spell and sharing your wealth indefinitely, in order to keep prosperity coming your way forever.

Chapter 9

Spells for Hard Times

Have you ever wondered why sometimes you seem to breeze through life, while other days nothing goes right? And why it is that when things start sliding downhill, they go from bad to worse? How can you keep the good times rolling and prevent the bad ones from getting a foothold? Is there a way to turn your luck around? Absolutely! That's what magick spells are for—to give you power over your destiny.

Affirmations for Difficult Times

No matter what misfortune befalls you or what dilemma you find yourself in, magick can help you deal with it. The spells in this chapter are designed to address a variety of problems, large and small. Many of them make use of tools and techniques that can be applied to just about any challenge. Others can be adapted for specific purposes simply by changing their ingredients so they relate to your intentions; the methodology remains the same.

During difficult times, we all need a little extra help staying positive. Try these affirmations to help keep your chin up. Write or type them out and post them where you will see them frequently.

1. I am now pulling in abundance and happiness.
2. My life is filled with great experiences.

3. I am grateful for all that I have.
4. I heal daily.
5. I give love freely.
6. I forgive and release.
7. I am moving forward with love and trust.

Piece of Cake Spell

When things aren't going as smoothly as you'd hoped—a project is costing more than expected; a romance has hit a snag; you have to deal with a lot of uncooperative people at work or at home—you might need some help to get through it. This spell uses Kitchen Witchery to sweeten a frustrating situation. Choose a flavor that suits your intentions: chocolate or strawberry for love; cinnamon or mint for money; almond or vanilla for peace of mind. You don't have to be a gourmet cook to carry off this spell—your intention is what counts. When you've finished baking your magick cake, you may want to share it with the other people who are involved in the challenging situation so that everyone benefits.

Tools:
A cake mix (or ingredients for making your favorite cake recipe)
Food coloring
A large bowl
A large spoon
Cake pan(s)
Candles
Matches or a lighter
When: Depends on your intentions (see Chapter 2)

Cast a Circle around the area where you will do your spell, in this case your kitchen. Preheat the oven.

Follow the directions for making the cake, according to the package or your favorite recipe. As you work, focus on your objective and imagine you are sending your intention into the batter. If you like, add food coloring to tint the batter to match your intention: pink for love, green for money, and so on. Stir the batter using a clockwise motion if your goal is to attract something or to stimulate an increase. Stir counterclockwise if you want to limit, decrease, or remove something. Pour the batter into the pan(s) and bake.

When the cake has finished cooking, let it cool. Ice it with frosting in a color that relates to your intention. You may want to decorate it with symbols, pictures, and words that also describe your objective. Add candles of an appropriate color. The number of candles should also correspond to your goal: two for love, four for stability, five for change, and so on.

Light the candles and concentrate on your wish. Blow out the candles. Share the cake with other people, if you like, or eat it yourself. Each person who partakes incorporates the intention into him- or herself and becomes a co-creator in the spell's success.

Salamander Courage Spell

Setbacks, disappointments, losses, or frustrating circumstances make you feel like giving up. In this spell you draw upon the fire power of the universe and solicit the assistance of the fire elementals to bolster your vitality and confidence.

Tools:
9 small red votive candles
Matches or a lighter
A magick wand
When: During the waxing moon, preferably on a Tuesday or when the sun and/or moon is in Aries, Leo, or Sagittarius

Arrange the candles in a Circle around you, in a place where you can safely leave them to burn down completely. Beginning in the east, light the candles one at a time as you move in a clockwise direction around the Circle. When all the candles are burning, stand in the center of the Circle and face south.

Call out to the salamanders, the elementals who inhabit the element of fire. Tell them you have lit these nine candles in their honor. Explain your situation and request their assistance, by chanting the following incantation aloud:

> *Beings of fire*
> *Shining so bright*
> *Fuel my desire*
> *Increase my might.*
> *Help me be strong*
> *All the day long*
> *So in every deed*
> *I'll surely succeed.*

You may notice faint flickerings of light—other than the candles—in the room or sense the energy around you quickening. It might even seem a bit warmer. That means the salamanders are present and willing to work with you. Take up your magick wand and point it toward the south. Envision yourself drawing powerful energy in through the tip of your wand. You might see the wand glow or feel it tingle.

Now turn the wand and aim it at yourself. Your movements should be strong and purposeful, not wimpy. Sense the energy you've attracted from the south—the region where the salamanders reside—flowing from the wand into your body. Feel yourself growing more powerful, more confident, more alive. Continue using your wand to pull energy and courage from the south in this manner for as long as you like.

Remain in the center of the Circle of candles until they have all burned down completely. Thank the salamanders for their assistance and leave the Circle with renewed vitality and confidence.

Deity Assistance Spell

Whatever your problem is, there's a deity who can help. This spell invokes divine assistance through burning incense. As the smoke rises, it carries your request into the heavens.

Tools:
A picture, figurine, or other image of your chosen deity
Incense
An incense burner
Matches or a lighter
A slip of paper
A pen or pencil
When: Depends on your intentions (see Chapter 2)

Determine which deity is best suited to help you with your problem. The tables in Chapter 1 list some well-known deities from around the world and the areas they govern. Once you've decided which deity to call upon, find an image/figurine of that god or goddess and display it on your altar.

Select an incense that corresponds to your intentions. Fit the incense into its burner and light it. Write your request on the slip of paper, fold it three times, and lay it at the feet of the deity. Envision your request floating up to the heavens, carried on the incense smoke to your chosen god or goddess.

Quiet your mind and listen for an answer or guidance. (Note: The answer may not come immediately—it could take a few days—so don't grow impatient.) Allow the incense to burn down completely. Thank the deity for helping you and trust that aid will come at the appropriate time.

Spell for Unexpected Expenses

When you least expect it, often at the most inopportune time, the dishwasher breaks or your car's air conditioner dies. Here's a spell to generate extra cash to cover those emergency expenses.

Tools:
Ballpoint pen
3 candles: one green, one gold, and one silver
3 candleholders
Enough coins to form a circle around all three candles (any denomination)
Matches or a lighter
When: Preferably during the waxing moon, but in an emergency you can do this spell as necessary

Using the ballpoint pen, carve the word *money* on the green candle. Inscribe the gold candle with the word *abundance* and write *now* on the silver candle.

Set the candles on your altar or another place where they can burn safely. Position them so they form a triangle, with the green and gold candles at the base and the silver one at the apex of the triangle. Next, make a circle around the candles with the coins. Make sure all the coins are face up and that each coin touches those on either side of it. Light the candles and call upon your favorite spiritual helper—a guardian angel, totem animal, or other deity—and ask for assistance in acquiring the money you need.

Allow the candles to burn down completely, but don't leave the burning candles unattended. If you must leave the altar before the candles finish burning, extinguish them and continue the spell later. When the candles have burned completely, thank the deity for helping you.

Quick Cash Potion

This magick potion starts working as soon as you ingest it. You can either brew this potion as a hot tea or enjoy it as a cool drink. If you like, share it with someone else whose intention to get fast cash is linked with your own.

Tools:
A sharp knife
Fresh ginger root
Fresh mint leaves
Spring water
Cinnamon
A clear glass or cup (no designs)
The ace of pentacles from a tarot deck or the ace of diamonds from a regular deck of playing cards
When: During the waxing moon, preferably on a Thursday, but in an emergency do the spell as necessary

Chop the ginger and mint leaves very finely—the amount is up to you. Sprinkle them in the spring water, then add a dash of cinnamon. If you wish, heat the water to make a tea (but don't let it boil). Pour the herb water into a clear glass or cup.

Lay the card face up on your altar, table, or countertop and set the glass of water on top of it. Leave it for five minutes to allow the image on the card to imprint the water with its vibrations. Then drink the water. If you like, repeat the spell each day until the cash you need arrives.

Amulet for Defense and Strength Against Creditors

Are annoying phone calls and demanding letters from collection agencies driving you nuts? This amulet gives you the courage and strength to weather the storm as you raise funds to pay off your debts.

Tools:
An image of a bear
The rune Eihwaz
A small piece of turquoise
Dried basil leaves
Dried fennel
Dried parsley
A black drawstring pouch, made of cloth or leather
When: During the waning moon, preferably on a Saturday

The image of a bear could be a magazine picture, a small figurine, a jewelry charm, or a drawing you sketch yourself. The rune Eihwaz, which means "defense," could be a piece of stone, ceramic, wood, or metal with the symbol carved or painted on it. (It looks a bit like a reversed Z tilted slightly clockwise.) Wash the turquoise with mild soap and water, then pat it dry.

Place the herbs, rune, and piece of turquoise in the pouch. Then hold the image of the bear in your hand and gaze at it. The bear represents protection and fortitude. Ask the spirit bear, symbolized by this image, to defend you and to give you the strength to "bear up" under the challenge you are facing. Add the bear to your pouch and close the pouch. Wear the amulet or carry it with you while you continue resolving your financial issues.

Lost Wallet Spell

You reach for your wallet and realize it's not there. But before you panic and let your imagination run wild, stop and perform this quick-and-easy spell.

When: As needed

Close your eyes, take a few slow, deep breaths, and calm yourself. In your mind's eye see your wallet (or purse) clearly. Now visualize a ball of pure white light completely surrounding your wallet, encasing it safely inside. Imagine your money, credit cards, driver's license, and so on tucked securely in place. Say or think the following affirmation:

My wallet and its contents are safe and sound.
They are returned to me now.

You may also wish to ask your favorite deity to help you locate the lost wallet or to intervene if it's been stolen. (Of course, you'll want to notify credit card companies and authorities promptly, especially if your wallet could have been missing for a while and you just noticed it.)

A Light in the Darkness

Let's say people aren't paying attention to you or giving your ideas the credence they deserve. Perhaps it's because they can't see the real you. This spell makes them sit up and take notice, as you shine your light into the darkness like a beacon.

Tools:
7 purple candles in candleholders
A tarot card that represents you (from a deck you don't normally use for readings)
Matches or a lighter
When: Begin seven days before the full moon

Choose a card from a tarot deck according to the chart in Chapter 4 to represent you in this spell. Lay the card face up on your altar or another spot where you can leave the spell components safely in place for a week. Arrange the candles in a tight circle around the card. Light the candles, starting with the candle at the top of the card and working your way around the circle in a clockwise direction until you've lit them all. Gaze at the setup for a few moments while you imagine yourself illuminated brilliantly, as if standing in a spotlight. See other people watching and admiring you. When you feel ready, extinguish the candles in a counterclockwise direction.

The next day, repeat the ritual. This time, however, widen the circle of candles by moving each candle out an inch or two. Repeat the ritual for a total of seven days, moving the candles apart a little more each day. As the circle of candles increases in size, you expand your personal power. The light you shine into the world burns brighter and touches more people. On the night of the full moon allow the candles to finish burning down completely.

Charm Bracelet

When you were a kid you may have worn a charm bracelet replete with tiny symbols that represented your interests or achievements. The symbols on this charm bracelet, however, represent your desires and intentions. Keeping these symbols in your immediate energy field makes this bracelet work, well, like a charm.

Tools:
A silver or gold link bracelet
Small charms that can be attached to the bracelet
When: Any time

Choose a bracelet that appeals to you and that can hold as many charms as you have wishes. You might want to wear a metal that harmonizes with your modus operandi. Silver embodies feminine qualities and corresponds to the moon. Its energy is receptive, intuitive, and emotional, and it works through the power of attraction. Gold signifies masculine qualities and relates to the sun. Its energy is active, direct, and logical, and it works through the power of assertion.

Select charms that hold meaning for you and that depict your objectives. If your goal is to attract a lover, a heart is an apt symbol. A car or airplane might represent travel. It's okay to combine talismans (to attract things you desire) with amulets (to repel things you prefer to keep at bay). Wear as many charms as you like. Add or remove them over time as your intentions change. Remember to wash your charms before wearing them, to get rid of any lingering energies left behind by other people who may have touched them.

Aladdin's Lamp

Remember the fable about the boy Aladdin who found a magick lamp with a genie inside? Like the genie in the story, this spell grants you three wishes to turn bad days into good ones.

Tools:
Incense
A metal oil lamp or a covered incense burner
Matches or a lighter
When: Depends on your intentions (see Chapter 2)

Use an old-fashioned oil lamp made of brass, tin, copper, or silver if you can find one; otherwise, substitute an incense burner with a lid that has perforations in it to allow the smoke to float out. Fit the incense into the lamp or incense burner and light it. Put the lid on so the smoke rises from the spout or perforations. Hold your hands on either side of the lamp/incense burner (don't actually touch it if the sides are hot) and pretend to rub it. Envision the smoke as a powerful genie who has come to do your bidding. You might even see a figure form in the smoke.

State your three wishes aloud as affirmations. In your mind's eye, see them already coming true. Spend a few minutes focusing on your requests as you inhale the scent of the incense.

Grace Under Fire Potion

If demands are flying at you from all directions at once and you feel like you're under siege, you may feel overwhelmed. Instead of caving in under the pressure, drink this magick potion to keep your cool.

Tools:
The Temperance card from a tarot deck
Spring water
A clear glass bottle (no designs) with a top or stopper
A few drops of Rescue Remedy (available in health food stores and some supermarkets)
A blue cloth
A chalice
When: As needed

Lay the Temperance card face up on your altar, table, or other surface. Fill the bottle with spring water and add a few drops of Rescue Remedy. Set the bottle on top of the card. Cover it with the cloth. Let it sit for at least ten minutes, to allow the image on the card to imprint the water in the bottle.

Uncover the bottle and put the tarot card back in the deck. Pour a little water into your chalice. Sip it slowly, allowing it to calm your nerves and restore your sense of balance. Store the remaining water in the refrigerator until you need it again. Repeat this spell as necessary to maintain your serenity and poise during stressful situations.

(Note: Don't eat or drink anything else for at least fifteen minutes before or after ingesting this magick potion.)

Clear the Air

This is a good ritual to try if an argument or upsetting experience has left bad vibes in your living space. To rid your home of the disruptive energy, perform this cleansing ritual.

Tools:
A broom
A bowl
Water
Sea salt
Sage (bundled, loose, or incense)
A fireproof holder that you can carry easily
Matches or a lighter
When: Any time

If possible, open the windows and doors. Start sweeping your home with a broom—not just the floor, but the air as well. Wave the broom through the entire area, side to side, up and down, until you feel you've whisked away the emotional "dirt." Next, fill a bowl with water and add a pinch of sea salt. Sprinkle a little in each corner of your home, then flick some water in the center of each room. Finally, put the sage into the holder and light it. Blow out the flames and let it smoke. Carry the burning sage from room to room, allowing its cleansing smoke to clear the air and restore peace to your home.

No Worries Incantation

You've got troubles on your mind, but worrying never makes things better. This spell uses the power of sound plus intention to chase fearful thoughts away and raise positive energy.

Tools:
A dark blue candle
A candleholder
Matches or a lighter
A hand drum or gong
An athame or wand
A bell
When: At midnight, during the waning moon

Fit the candle in its holder, set it on your altar (or other surface where it can burn safely), and light it. Begin playing the drum or gong to break up negative thoughts and vibrations. Feel the sound resonating through you, too, stirring up your power and confidence. When you feel ready, chant the following incantation aloud. If possible, shout it out—really assert yourself!

> *Doubt and fear*
> *Don't come near.*
> *By the dawn*
> *Be you gone.*
> *By this sign [with your athame or wand draw a pentagram in the air in front of you]*
> *And light divine*
> *Peace is mine.*
> *I am strong*
> *All day long.*
> *My worries flee*
> *Magickally.*
> *I ring this bell [ring the bell]*
> *To bind this spell,*
> *And all is well.*

As you chant, envision your fears receding into the darkness, losing their strength. When you're ready, extinguish the candle.

Spell to Overcome an Obstacle

A daunting challenge looms before you, stymieing you with its magnitude. Instead of giving up, call in some extra muscle to help you handle the task. Since ancient times, the people of India have drawn upon the strength of the elephant god Ganesh to help them overcome seemingly insurmountable obstacles. So can you.

Tools:
An image of an elephant or of Ganesh (for example, a magazine photo or small figurine)
An athame (or kitchen knife)
When: On a Saturday, or when the sun and/or moon is in Capricorn

Place your image of Ganesh on your altar. Close your eyes and imagine you're in a dark, dense jungle. The vegetation is so thick you can see only a foot or two ahead of you. All sorts of dangers lurk unseen. You feel trapped and helpless. The tangled vines and thick overgrowth represent the obstacles facing you.

Suddenly, you hear the trumpeting call of an elephant—it's Ganesh coming to your rescue. Pick up your athame (or kitchen knife). Without hesitation he rushes toward you and easily lifts you with his trunk onto his back. Explain to him the nature of your problem. Visualize yourself riding on Ganesh's back as he marches into the jungle, trampling everything in his path.

Reach out with your athame and begin slashing away at the vines and branches, hacking through the obstacles. See space opening up before you. Feel Ganesh's strength, lifting you high above your problems. Together you are unstoppable. Keep chopping away at the thick vegetation, eliminating obstacles one by one. When you feel ready, climb down from Ganesh's back and thank him for his assistance. Repeat as necessary.

Knotty Situation Spell

A stressful situation has you all tied up in knots. This spell uses the symbolism of knots to help you get out the kinks and release tension.

Tools:
A piece of cord or rope as long as your spine
Matches or a lighter
When: During the waning moon

Choose a piece of cord or rope in a color that represents your dilemma: green for money woes, pink for troubles in love, and so on. Tie several knots in the rope to represent difficulties. These signify the areas where you feel bound by problems.

When you're ready, slowly untie one knot. Envision the tension in the situation easing as you loosen the knot. Feel your mind begin to relax and let go of the problem. Untie another knot and visualize another blockage being removed. See or sense your heart and mind opening up, becoming more receptive and less rigid. Keep untying the knots one at a time. Don't hurry; work at your own pace. With each knot, a problem or a facet of the overall problem is resolved.

As you continue opening the knots you may receive ideas about how to handle the difficulties represented by the knots or gain deeper insight into your own role in the problem. When you've finished untying all the knots, breathe a sigh of relief and let yourself feel calm, confident, and untroubled. Burn the rope in a safe place.

Signs of the Times

Confusion reigns and you don't know where to turn for advice. If only the universe would give you a sign! Well, maybe you just need to open your eyes. Long ago Celtic prognosticators known as frithir read the signs of the times from the first thing that caught their attention when they stepped outside. Try this ancient divination technique to get the guidance you need.

When: The first Monday after a solstice or equinox

Immediately after arising in the morning—before you do anything else—sit quietly for a few minutes and contemplate the situation that has you in a quandary. Then go to your door and close your eyes. Take three slow, deep breaths before opening the door. Open the door and step outside, if you can do this safely with your eyes closed. Otherwise, just stand in the open doorway facing out. Open your eyes. What's the first thing you see? What significance does it hold for you? A squirrel could suggest that you get busy gathering money, information, or other resources. A butterfly might mean a change is coming.

Notice any impressions or feelings that arise into your awareness—they may be significant. If you don't sense an immediate answer, simply tuck away the memory of what you've seen and allow it to percolate in your subconscious. You might want to do some research into classic symbolism associated with the object that caught your attention. Pretty soon, perhaps in a dream, you'll receive the guidance you've been seeking.

Don't Give Up Spell

When nothing seems to be going right, this spell helps you hang in there until the situation improves.

> *Tools:*
> Oak flower essence (available in health food stores or online)
> A piece of yellow paper
> A pen or marker with red ink
> A black candle
> A candleholder
> Matches or a lighter
> A tarot card that represents you (see Chapter 4)
> The Strength tarot card (which signifies inner and outer strength)
> The seven of wands tarot card (which represents the ability to hold firm when you're challenged or attacked)
> The Star tarot card (which symbolizes hope)
> The World tarot card (which indicates everything working out successfully)
> *When:* Daily

Put a few drops of oak flower essence under your tongue. On the paper, draw a red pentagram at least one foot in diameter. Lay it face up on your altar, a table, or another flat surface where it can remain for a period of time. Fit the candle in its holder and set it in the center of the pentagram. Light the candle.

Place the tarot card that represents you on the top point of the pentagram. Position the cards Strength and the seven of wands on the two side points of the pentagram. Put the Star and the World cards on the pentagram's bottom two points. Gaze at the cards and allow their symbolism to imprint your subconscious with positive imagery. Feel them stimulating the courage and confidence you need to face the challenges before you. When you feel ready or start to lose your focus, extinguish the candle. Repeat this spell daily, for as long as necessary.

Cauldron Dream Manifestation Spell

A particular wish probably won't materialize overnight; it's going to take a while to develop. While you're waiting, cast this spell to nurture your dreams and bring them to fruition. Your patience will help you through the tough time.

Tools:
A sheet of paper
Scissors
A pen or pencil
A cauldron (or other bowl-shaped container)
Powdered ginger
Blessed thistle (dried herb, capsules, or tablets)
A green cloth
When: The day after the new moon

Cut the sheet of paper into twelve strips. On one strip write your wish in the form of an affirmation. Fold the paper strip three times and put it in the cauldron. Sprinkle a little powdered ginger in the cauldron (to speed up results) and a little blessed thistle (to help your goal manifest). Simply open a capsule or grind a tablet into powder, then add it to the cauldron. Cover the cauldron with the green cloth.

Allow the spell to "simmer" overnight, then in the morning remove the cloth and repeat the spell. Continue in this manner for a total of twelve days. If your wish hasn't materialized by the time of the full moon, take a break during the waning moon period and begin again on the first day of the waxing moon. Don't give up—trust that your wish will indeed manifest when the time is right.

A Spell to Get Rid of Old Baggage

Are old habit patterns, fears, and outdated attitudes getting in the way of your success? This spell helps you eliminate old baggage so it doesn't keep weighing you down.

Tools:
A piece of paper
A pen or pencil
A cauldron or other fireproof container
Matches or a lighter
When: During the waning moon

On the paper, write down whatever it is you want to eliminate from your life. Describe how this old baggage is limiting you. If you like, explore what you believe to be the root of the condition. Allow your emotions to come up and write about how you feel.

When you've finished, read what you've written. Then crumple the paper loosely, light it, and drop it in the cauldron. As the paper burns, envision your old baggage burning up, too. When the paper has completely burned, allow the ashes to cool. Take the ashes to a cemetery. Say aloud:

This old part of my life is dead and gone, and I am now free of its influence.

Scatter the ashes in the wind.

A Step in the Right Direction

This spell might sound a little silly, but a lighthearted approach is sometimes best when dealing with everyday troubles. Don't be put off by the playful quality of the spell—it can be quite powerful.

> *Tools:*
> Nail polish
> Polish remover
> Cotton balls and/or swabs
> *When:* Depends on your intentions

Select one or more bottles of nail polish, in colors that correspond to your intentions: pink or red for love, green or gold for money, and so on. Assign an objective to each toe. You can give all ten toes the same intention or pick ten different goals—or any other combination. Begin painting your toenails in colors that are appropriate to your objectives. As you paint each nail, concentrate on your intention and envision it already manifesting. If you like, decorate your nails with symbols that represent your intentions: dollar signs for money, hearts for love, and so on. Have fun and be creative. If you make a mistake or change your mind, simply remove the polish and start over.

Allow the polish to dry. For the next week or so, or for as long as the polish lasts, each step you take will bring you closer to your goals.

Guardian Angel Charm

Challenging situations often seem bigger than you can handle. According to many spiritual traditions, everyone has a personal guardian angel who is always there to provide guidance and protection. This magick charm reminds you that your angelic helper is near at hand.

Tools:
A small silver or gold hanging charm in the shape of an angel
A white cord or ribbon 18 inches long
Essential oil of amber
When: On a Saturday

Slide the charm onto the cord or ribbon and tie a knot to make a pendant necklace. As you tie the knot, envision yourself safe, happy, and healthy. Say the following incantation aloud:

Guardian angel, be with me.
Keep me healthy, safe, and free.
Guide my steps so I may see
What I must do. Blessed be.

Put a dot of amber essential oil on the angel charm. Inhale the scent and let it calm your nerves. You may sense your guardian angel nearby. Envision yourself placing your concerns in the angel's hands, knowing that everything will be taken care of. Slip the necklace over your head and wear it for protection.

Guardian Angel Ritual
Here's another way to request angelic assistance and protection. With this ritual you move up a rung in the heavenly hierarchy to call upon the archangels: Raphael, Michael, Gabriel, and Uriel. Perform this ritual alone to petition their aid, or do it in conjunction with other spells.

Tools:
A yellow votive candle
A red votive candle
A blue votive candle
A green votive candle

Matches or a lighter
When: Any time

Stand facing east and set the yellow candle on the ground (or floor) in front of you, where it can burn safely. Light the candle and say aloud:

Archangel Raphael, Guardian of the East, come and be with me in this sacred space.
I request your protection and guidance in all I do, now and always.

Move clockwise until you are facing south, and set the red candle on the ground (or floor) in front of you. Light the candle and say aloud:

Archangel Michael, Guardian of the South, come and be with me in this sacred space.
I request your protection and guidance in all I do, now and always.

Move clockwise until you are facing west, and set the blue candle on the ground (or floor) in front of you. Light the candle and say aloud:

Archangel Gabriel, Guardian of the West, come and be with me in this sacred space.
I request your protection and guidance in all I do, now and always.

Move clockwise until you are facing north, and set the green candle on the ground (or floor) in front of you. Light the candle and say aloud:

Archangel Uriel, Guardian of the North, come and be with me in this sacred space.
I request your protection and guidance in all I do, now and always.

Stand in the center of the Circle you've cast. Close your eyes and envision the four archangels standing around you, like sentries protecting you from harm. Feel their power flowing into you, filling you with strength and confidence.

Remain in the center of the Circle for as long as you wish. If you like, you can perform another spell or ritual now, under the watchful guard of the archangels. When you are ready, open the Circle in the following manner. Go to the east and stand facing outward. Say aloud:

Archangel Raphael, Guardian of the East, I thank you for your presence here this night (or day).

Please continue to guide and protect me always and all ways, even after you return to your home in the heavens. Hail, farewell, and blessed be.

Extinguish the yellow candle. Move counterclockwise to the north and stand facing outward. Say aloud:

Archangel Uriel, Guardian of the North, I thank you for your presence here this night (or day).

Please continue to guide and protect me always and all ways, even after you return to your home in the heavens. Hail, farewell, and blessed be.

Extinguish the green candle. Go to the west and stand facing outward. Say aloud:

Archangel Gabriel, Guardian of the West, I thank you for your presence here this night (or day).

Please continue to guide and protect me always and all ways, even after you return to your home in the heavens. Hail, farewell, and blessed be.

Extinguish the blue candle. Go to the south and stand facing outward. Say aloud:

Archangel Michael, Guardian of the South, I thank you for your presence here this night (or day).

Please continue to guide and protect me always and all ways, even after you return to your home in the heavens. Hail, farewell, and blessed be.

Extinguish the red candle.

Yule Good Luck Charm

Would you like to help your friends and loved ones with their problems by boosting their good luck throughout the coming year? This Yuletide custom lets you make a unique magickal gift for everyone on your list that will help keep their hard times few and far between.

Tools:
A Yule log (usually oak)
Matches or a lighter
A cloth drawstring pouch for each friend/loved one on your gift list
Dried pink rose petals (for love)
Dried lavender buds or leaves (for peace of mind)
Dried basil (for protection)
Dried mint leaves (for prosperity)
Dried echinacea (for health)
A sheet of paper
Scissors
A pen
When: Yule (usually December 21)

On the night of the Winter Solstice, build a Yule fire in a safe place and burn an oak log in it. Allow the fire to burn down completely. The next morning when the ashes have cooled, scoop some into each pouch. Add the dried botanicals. Cut the sheet of paper into slips, one for each person on your list. Write a personalized wish on each slip of paper. Fold the papers three times and add them to the pouches. Tie the pouches closed and give them to your loved ones.

Chapter 10

Spells for Personal Power

Personal power has a lot to do with having presence. To have it, you don't need to be a movie star, writer, politician, celebrity, or anyone else in the public eye. In fact, your job or career really has nothing to do with it. This type of presence comes from within. There are kids who have it. There are elderly people who have it. You can encounter people from all walks of life who have it and, quite often, they don't even realize what they have. In some instances, a person may be born with presence, but usually it's something that must be cultivated, nurtured, explored. Usually, it's an ineffable quality that manifests over time, with the development of self-knowledge.

There it is again. That old adage. Know thyself.

To know yourself and to use what you learn requires an act of will. The dictionary definition of the word describes it as "choice, determination, volition." But what does any of that really mean?

The Power of Your Will

Your will is the crux of every visualization, manifestation, and spell. It's the act of galvanizing yourself at the deepest levels to achieve something that you desire. You don't simply say the words. You don't just go through the motions. You plunge into yourself, you delve, to discover your true motives, needs, and desires. You work to bring that self-knowledge to full consciousness, into your daily awareness. Then you commit to the path and trust the process.

⋇ **Wiccan Wonderings: What's the best way to build your store of personal power?**

To increase your personal power, first pinpoint which area of your life lacks power. Is it your professional life, love life, spiritual life, family life, or creative life? Once you determine which area you want to work on, redesign the Spell for Personal Empowerment to fit your needs. Refer to the material on ingredients to decide what to use in your spell. Do this spell during the full moon.

When you develop this sort of awareness, synchronicities tend to proliferate in your life and they often occur in clusters. More and more frequently, you may find that external events precisely mirror inner conditions. At the same time, your dreams might become especially vivid and cluster around one or two themes. Pay attention to these types of themes, as they are meant to help crystalize things and increase your understanding.

The spells that follow are intended to expand self-awareness and to enhance your willpower.

A Spell for Personal Empowerment

This spell requires no tools except the belief that magick works—and that it can work for you. This spell can be done quickly and can be done anywhere—not just as you're waking up in the morning. The most important ingredients are the vividness with which you visualize the end result and the intensity of the emotion behind your desire.

As you're waking up in the morning, before your eyes open, when you're still in that drowsy state halfway between dreams and full consciousness, visualize whatever it is that you desire. Then say it silently to yourself.

Maybe your desire is to ace an exam. Visualize it as vividly as possible, a big red A at the top of your exam sheet. Pour emotion into it.

Imagine how excited you'll be when you see the A. Then say, "I ace my exam." Again, put emotion behind the statement.

When you've done this with great vividness and backed it with emotion, then get out of bed and forget about it. Release the desire. Assuming that you've done your part to get an A on the exam (studied or otherwise prepared yourself), you should get an A.

A Spell to Expand Self-Awareness

Do this spell on a Thursday, because that's Jupiter's day and Jupiter symbolizes expansion. If you can't do it on a Thursday, then definitely do this during a full moon, on any day except Tuesday (Mars) or Saturday (Saturn). The object should be something solid and three-dimensional: a stone, for instance, versus a photograph. The crystal can be any color, but should be clear. It will amplify your desire.

Tools:
Frankincense oil
Myrrh oil
An amber-colored candle
Object that represents personal power
Quartz crystal
When: Preferably on a Thursday night during a full moon

Pick a spot where you won't be disturbed. If it's temperate where you are, this spell works nicely outside, under the light of the full moon. Put several drops of both oils into your burner and place it on your left. Put the amber-colored candle on your right. The object that represents your personal power and the crystal should go directly in front of you.

Light the candles, then throw open your arms to the moon. Vividly imagine its light suffusing you and say:

This light is presence,
This light is power.

It fills me
Until I am presence,
Until I am power.

Allow the aroma of the oils to permeate the air, then pinch out the flames. Place your power object in a safe place. You may want to let your crystal soak in saltwater overnight to cleanse it. Or, you can leave it outside where the light of the full moon will charge it.

Brave Heart Lotion

You have to make an appearance before someone—or a group of people—who you fear can't wait to shoot you down. Instead of worrying that they will judge you harshly, concoct this magick lotion. It protects you from attack by bolstering your courage.

Tools:
A small carnelian or ruby
A glass jar or bottle, preferably amber-colored, with a lid or stopper
8 ounces almond oil
3 drops amber essential oil
3 drops cedar essential oil
¼ teaspoon dried basil leaves
When: Several days before your appearance, preferably on a Tuesday or Sunday; if you don't have that much time, do the spell as needed

Wash the gemstone and the bottle/jar with mild soap and water. Pour the almond oil into the bottle/jar. Add the essential oils and inhale the fragrance, allowing it to invigorate your mind. Crumble the basil leaves very finely and add them to the oil. Add the gemstone. Cap the bottle/jar and shake it three times to blend and charge the ingredients.

Each morning, pour a little of the magick oil into your palm and dip your index finger in it. Then rub the oil on your skin at your heart center. Feel it strengthening your confidence. Take several slow, deep breaths, letting the scent strengthen and vitalize you. Repeat each morning until your fear diminishes. Rub a little extra on your chest immediately before you must face the critics.

Evil Eye Amulet

Do you feel you're under attack? Since ancient times, people in cultures around the world have used eye amulets to ward off evil of all kinds. Whether the evil force threatening you is human, animal, or supernatural, this all-seeing protection charm guards your home and its inhabitants.

> *Tools:*
> A disk of wood, ceramic, or stone about 1½ inches in diameter
> Blue, black, and white paint
> A small paintbrush
> A white ribbon at least 1 inch wide and 4 to 6 inches long
> Tacky glue or something to attach the disk to the ribbon
> A small loop or hook for hanging
> Other adornments (optional)
> *When:* On a Saturday

Paint a blue eye on the disk—make it realistic or stylized. If you like, decorate the ribbon with symbols or designs that represent protection to you, such as pentagrams or circles. When the paint dries, attach the disk to the top of the ribbon.

Affix the loop or hook to the back of the disk. Hang the amulet inside your home, near the front door. Each time you enter or leave your home, touch the eye amulet for good luck and to reinforce your intention.

A Spell for Sexual Charisma

As an herb, rue strengthens willpower, sage is excellent for mental clarity and protection and a general cleansing of negative energy, and mint speeds up the results of a spell. You can also consult the lists of herbs in this book and add any others that you feel are appropriate. Tuesday is ruled by Mars, which governs sexual energy. Jupiter, as Thursday's ruler, means expansion, luck. If you're casting this spell in the hopes of seducing someone, then one of the candle colors should be red. Allow your intuition to guide you on the other three colors.

Tools:
Abalone shell
Rue, the herb
Sage, incense or herb
Mint
4 candles, your choice of colors
When: Preferably a Tuesday or a Thursday on a full moon. If neither of those days is possible, then a Friday or Sunday would be fine, too.

Place the herbs in the abalone shell. Light the sage, rue, and mint first, so their scent permeates the air where you're working. Next, light the candles. As you light each one, imagine your sexuality and your charisma burning brightly during the time that you need it to do whatever you're going to do!

The Flow

"The flow" is one of the millennial buzzwords and usually has "go with" preceding it, as in "Go with the flow." The biggest problem with this phrase is that it implies passivity. It seems to be saying that if we don't do anything, if we just wait for things to unfold, we're going with the flow. In actuality, the flow is like a current made up of synchronicities. It's up to us to figure out what these often odd connections mean, what their deeper significance is, and in doing so, we're able to determine the direction and purpose of the flow. This in itself is empowering. We feel as if we're hooked into something larger than ourselves, that the bigger picture is vastly more complex than we dared imagine.

The flow of a river is altered constantly by the curvature of the land that contains it, weather patterns, and myriad other environmental details. In the same way, the purpose of the flow in our lives changes as our goals and needs change. By developing an awareness of this deeper stratum of our lives, we're better equipped to anticipate opportunities, deal with challenges, and fulfill our potential. In short, we are empowered.

A Spell for Empowering the Energy Centers

This spell is quick and simple. It only requires that you bring your intent and your belief to the spell. It is designed for the first energy center, or chakra (see Chapter 7), but can be modified to work for the others as well.

Tools:
4 red candles
Matches or a lighter
When: A Friday night on the full moon

Place the four candles at the four cardinal directions. Starting at the north, move clockwise to light the candles. With each candle that you light, imagine your first center as a swirling orb of strong, pulsating energy that imbues your being with sexual charisma and power.

When you have finished lighting the candles, spend a few minutes in the center of your candle Circle, preferably in the lotus position. Inhale deeply several times, then exhale quickly, expelling all the air from your lungs. Pinch your right nostril shut, inhale through the left, and hold for a count of ten. Exhale through the right nostril. Repeat five times and switch sides. As you do this alternate nostril breathing, imagine your first energy center imbued with power.

This spell can be repeated with each of the centers, using the appropriate colors. When you feel comfortable casting spells, you can create your own rhyme for each of the cardinal directions, to say when you light the candles.

Stretching Your Energy Field

People who have presence, who have personal power, often have an expanded energy field or aura as well. The energy field, in fact, is what we react to when that person walks into our view. With practice, you can learn to expand your energy field from the usual several inches around your body to several feet. The field is easy to detect through touch. Stand in front of a mirror and open your arms wide, as if you're about to hug someone. Bring your hands slowly toward your head until you feel a slight resistance. This should happen when your hands are several inches away from your head. When your energy field expands, you'll feel the resistance farther away from your head.

You can also train yourself to see your energy field. Gaze into a mirror in a twilit room. It's best if a dim light is at your back. If you wear glasses or contacts, remove them. If you have 20/20 vision, gaze at your head in the mirror and let your eyes unfocus, so that your reflection seems hazy. The longer you gaze at your reflection in this way, the more likely you are to see a halo of light surrounding your head. Some people detect colors, others simply see a halo of transparent light. Now think of something that made you exceptionally happy—your marriage, the birth of your child, the purchase of your first home, getting an offer for a great job. Conjure the emotions that you felt during this event or experience. Let the emotion fill you completely. As the emotions suffuse your entire being, your energy field will start to expand, and the halo will balloon.

As you're feeling your energy field expand, take several deep breaths. Pinch your right nostril shut and breathe in through your left nostril. Hold your breath for a count of ten and exhale through your right nostril. Repeat three times, then switch nostrils. Alternate nostril breathing stimulates both hemispheres of the brain and, as you become accustomed to charging your energy field, the alternate breathing signals your unconscious of your intent.

With practice, you can charge your energy field in ten or fifteen seconds. You can use this technique for just about anything—when you're hoping to attract love, new job opportunities, or meet new friends. Your body becomes the tool. It can be done anywhere, anytime.

Chapter 11

Spells for Creativity

In its broadest definition, "creativity" is the act of coming up with something new rather than producing an imitation. We tend to think of creativity as applying only to certain areas of life, such as arts or inventions, but in reality, creativity belongs to all aspects of life.

All of us are inherently creative. We all come up with new ways of doing things, new ideas, new approaches, new perspectives and insights. Our right brains are tireless workers. They churn out ideas twenty-four hours a day, every day, every year of our lives. Part of our problem, however, is that we're creatures of habit. If something has worked in the past, we keep following that groove because it takes less effort—and besides, who wants to mess with success? We begin to approach living from some sort of internal formula. If we do A, then we do B and C all the way through Z, even though it might feel old and tired. Then we sit up one day and realize with a certain growing horror that we have fallen into a rut.

Are You in a Rut?

If you feel like you're in a rut, use the following brainstorming questions as a springboard to provide insight into your own creative process, what you need to alter to become more creative, and what your ultimate creative goals are.

1. If you could do anything with your life, what would it be?
2. What are your hobbies, and why?
3. Do you consider your hobbies creative? Why or why not?
4. Do you consider yourself creative?
5. What do you consider the most creative part of your life and why?
6. Do you feel as if you're in a rut in any area of your life? If so, are you willing to change it?
7. Describe your rut.
8. What do you think you can do to change it? If it's a job, are you willing to change jobs? If it's a relationship, are you willing to reassess it or get out of it?
9. What's the first step you would take to get out of the rut?
10. How can you apply your creative talents in another area of your life to get out of that rut?

Breaking Out of Your Rut

Let's say you're stuck in a rut at work. You hate your job, but at the moment you don't have any other prospects on the horizon. Even so, you're preparing a résumé, putting out feelers, and setting things in motion. In the meantime, you can do some simple magick, and it starts with nothing more than taking a different route to and from work. On the first morning that you take the new route, give yourself some extra time. Leave ten or fifteen minutes earlier than usual. Notice how this route to work differs from the one you ordinarily take. Is it more scenic? More hectic? Is it longer or shorter? Take note of any feelings you have during the drive, any thoughts and insights that surface. Throughout your day at work, notice if you feel differently about your job. Are you more committed to finding something else to do? Are your thoughts any clearer? Does your boss still rub you the wrong way?

Even by changing something as minor as this, you're breaking out of your habitual ways of doing things. Once you change your drive to work, you can start doing other small, routine tasks in your work and home life differently. Changing old patterns and ways of thinking serves as a symbolic gesture to the universe that you're ready for change. Never underestimate the power of change—with new dreams, you can create a new life.

✳ **Wiccan Wonderings: What, exactly, is a creative muse, and how can you get in touch with it?**

The creative muse is nearly always spoken of as "she." But a muse can also be a "he" or have no gender at all. It can simply be energy that you name, as you might a beloved pet. To get in touch with your muse, simply put out the request: Write it in your Book of Shadows; tell yourself as you're falling asleep that you're going to communicate with your muse in a dream; meditate on it; or even write your muse a note.

A Spell to Change Outmoded Patterns

Once you've identified the patterns you want to change in your life, make one small gesture that expresses your intent.

> *Tools:*
> A piece of paper
> A pen with ink in a color that represents your desire
> 2 sets of 2 candles, in colors that represent your desire
> A power object
> Abalone shell
> *When:* On the first and seconds nights of the full moon

On the first night of the full moon, jot down your desire on a sheet of paper, in ink of a color that seems appropriate for what you want. For instance, if your wish is to be more creative with your financial investments, then use green ink. Or, if you want to be more creative in your professional life, use gold ink. Then light two candles of a close or matching color and read your wish out loud three times. Back the words with emotion—say them as if you mean them. Tuck your written desire under a power object and let the candles burn out naturally.

On the second night of the full moon, light two more candles of the same color. Repeat your wish three times. Then touch the paper to one of the flames and say:

As this paper is burning,
I release my wish, my need,
My deepest yearnings,
A new life's seed.

Put the burning paper in the abalone shell. When the second set of candles has burned out on its own, toss it out.

A Spell to Enhance Creativity

Choose something that represents the area of your life where you would like to enhance or increase your creativity. Any object or symbol will do. Keep it in a place where you'll see it daily.

Feel the words as you think them. Feel your changing beliefs. Then, make a gesture that's connected to your creativity at least once a day for a month.

Creativity and Dreams

Dream books are filled with stories about how a dream provided the missing piece of an invention, vital scenes in a novel, the finishing touches of a movie, or some unique image in a painting. Dreams are so intimately connected to creativity and to the creative process that to ignore them or to write them off as merely pleasant interludes is to cheat yourself.

The fodder dreams provide comes to each of us in unique ways. Some dreams are symbolic, others are literal. Some are ordinary, others are bizarre. Some are fun, some are terrifying. Regardless of the particularities in which a dream is couched, it is your dream, intimately connected to the creative process that churns inside of you every day of your life.

Dreams are the conduit through which we connect to each other and to the deeper, oceanic parts of ourselves. Within that vast inner ocean are buried creative seeds that may never sprout unless we bring them into the light of day. Dreams, by their fundamental nature, are magick.

Here are a few guidelines on how to recall your dreams and work with them to enhance your creativity:

- **Voice what you need or want.** Before you fall asleep at night, say aloud that you would like to remember the most important dreams of the night. If you're trying to find a particular solution to something, then request that an answer come to you in a dream that you'll remember in detail.
- **Back up your request with a gesture.** Put a recorder by your bedside or slide a notebook under your pillow so that you can immediately record what you remember when you wake up. You might even jot your request on a page in your journal. Date it. Make notes the next day about whether you remembered any dreams. Sometimes the act of trying to write about your dreams when you're sure you haven't remembered any is enough to trigger recall.
- **Pay attention.** Any dream fragment that you remember may relate to your request even if it doesn't appear to do so. Don't judge it. Forget your left-brain censor. Just write down the fragment. Record it.
- **If you don't succeed at first, keep trying.** Yes, it's a cliché. It also happens to be true. If you've spent thirty or forty years forgetting the bulk of what goes on while you sleep, then you can bet the remembering wheels are rusty. Oil them and keep making your requests. Sooner or later, you'll have a powerful, significant dream, and you'll remember the characters, the texture, the nuances.
- **Experiment.** If you don't seem to be remembering any dreams or your requests don't appear to be working, then sleep elsewhere

for a couple of nights. On the couch. In a sleeping bag. At your mother's place. When we break the rut we're in by changing a habit, new things unfold.

All of this might not sound like spellwork, but it is. You are bringing your intent, will, emotions, and anything else you can muster to get a creative solution to your request. It's visualization in another form.

"My safest place is in my dreams," writes Judith Orloff in *Intuitive Healing*. "There I become centered. I inhabit a form that feels more fluid, and I effortlessly replenish myself with images, energy, tones that are a bigger stretch to accommodate otherwise." Maybe that's the key. Each of us must befriend our dreams, must approach them as though they are old friends who will listen to us and offer a fresh perspective on whatever we're looking for or need.

A Ritual to Bring about Vivid Dreams

This ritual can be done in various ways depending on your preferences.

> *Tools:*
> Comforting food or drink (see directions)
> Sprig of vervain
> *When:* At bedtime

Create a ritual for going to bed. Have a cup of chamomile tea, a glass of milk, or a bowl of ice cream beforehand. Treat yourself to a food or drink from which you derive comfort, the kind of comfort that your parents gave you when you were a kid, preparing to go to bed.

Place a sprig of vervain under your pillow, next to your dream journal or Book of Shadows—it promotes vivid dreams. So do the color blue, the scent of cedar (incense or oil), a warm bath, and the sound of water. Try sleeping in blue sheets with a few drops of cedar oil on them. Set up a small fountain so it will sound like the gentle caress of the ocean surf against a beach. Sometimes, the whisper of wind is invaluable. Do something that soothes each of your senses.

As you get into bed, state your request. Spend a few minutes reading or doing whatever relaxes you. As you turn out the light, repeat your request, and trust that it will be answered.

Practical Creativity

This might sound like an oxymoron, but creativity is always practical. It's the perfect blend of right and left brain. What the right brain can conceive, the left brain can put into action. If your creative impetus feels sluggish and you can't seem to get to first base with spells, dreams, or anything else, then maybe it's time to take a back-door approach and do some left-brain defining. The creative process begs for a structure. Give me a goal, it pleads. Give me a backbone. And if you can't do that, then at least give me a deadline.

A deadline often provides the badly needed backbone for creativity. The advertising executive needs three spots for tomorrow's slot at 8 A.M. The reporter needs to call in his story at noon. The gallery needs two paintings for this week's exhibit. Forget dreams. Forget visualizations. Forget the tools that have worked before. You need a product and you need it now.

At such times, the creativity god slams into overdrive. It plucks up this remnant from sixth grade and that vague memory from the day your mother died and tosses in the color purple and a scent of pine. It squeezes all these seemingly disparate pieces into the backbone your left brain created and suddenly you have a product. You have an answer. You have a solution.

Left brain, right brain. The difference, on the surface, is nothing more than hemispheres and directions. The left brain, the experts tell us, is good at math and reasoning, good at minutia and connecting the dots. The right brain excels at seeing the whole picture. Neither is better than the other. We need both. We can't survive if the signal from one is very weak or very strong. We need a balance between the two, and it doesn't matter which one takes the lead. Creativity rises from a perfect blend between left brain and right.

A Spell to Balance the Hemispheres

This breathing exercise, used in certain yoga traditions, balances both hemispheres of the brain, allowing them to work smoothly together. It allows them to talk to each other. And that talk, that private conversation they have, is essential to any creative process.

When: Any time

Before you dive into a creative project, find a comfortable spot anywhere, shut the door, and sit on the floor, with your back against a wall. Hold your left nostril shut and breathe through the right. Hold it for a count of ten and exhale forcefully through your mouth. Repeat this three times, then switch sides and repeat three times.

Once you get the hang of it, you can do this breathing exercise anywhere, anytime.

Calling on Nature to Boost Creativity

What if you've tried all of that alternate breathing stuff, and you've worked at your dream recall, but nothing's panned out? You're still so entrenched in your rut that you can feel its walls collapsing around you.

Then it's time for a break. Put on your sneakers and head for the great outdoors—the best scenario is a place without conveniences within fifteen or twenty miles. In lieu of that, find a green place that is moderately private.

Wild Animals and the Creative Spark

When you run across an animal in the wild, you are seized by an archetypal energy of freedom and instinct. Depending on the circumstances and the type of animal, you might be seized by fear as well. But even fear can galvanize your creativity. The vividness of even the briefest encounters with wild animals stays with you, and it can trigger all sorts of creative thoughts and images.

When you get outside, observe the wildlife. Enjoy the smell of the air, the firmness of the ground under your feet. And take note of how your thought processes start to change. You'll have to put up with your internal grumblings at first. You know, the usual complaints: It's too far, I'm hot, I'm thirsty, I'm hungry, where's the bathroom, and so on. But when you get past all that—and you will—something magickal happens. You can almost feel the inner shift.

Your thoughts begin to flow rather than to sputter. Your rhythm changes. Your gait quickens or slows. You feel lighter, happier, more optimistic. And this is exactly the right atmosphere for your creativity to percolate. Quite often, when you venture into nature simply to see what you'll discover, your creativity is stimulated in unusual and, sometimes, enduring ways.

Feng Shui Spell to Enhance Creativity

To locate the area of your home that corresponds to creativity, stand at the doorway that you use most often to enter or exit your home, facing in. Halfway between the furthest right-hand corner and the nearest right-hand corner is the sector known as the creativity gua.

Tools:
An affirmation written on a slip of paper
3 coins
A bowl
Yellow rose petals
When: When the moon is waxing, in Leo or Libra

Write an affirmation on a slip of paper, describing your intention. Remember to state it in the present tense. For example, you might write, "A major publishing company now buys my novel and I am content with all aspects of the contract." Or you could state, "I now land a role in the upcoming community play" or, "My tulips win an award in the spring gardening show."

Place your written affirmation in the creativity sector of your home, then position the three coins on top of it. The coins symbolize receiving money (or other rewards) for your creativity. Next, set the bowl on top of the coins and the affirmation. The bowl, a variation of the chalice (discussed in Chapter 4), represents receptivity and your willingness to attract and hold onto creative ideas. Fill the bowl with the rose petals. Yellow, the color associated with creativity and self-esteem, suggests that your creative ideas are blossoming and taking shape in the material world. Leave this spell in place until the full moon or until your wish materializes.

A Practical Spell to Sell

Talk about creativity and animals, creativity and dreams, and creativity and nature is all well and good, but if you have a specific goal, you need to make it practical. Do you have a screenplay that needs to find its way to the right people? Paintings or photographs that deserve to be exhibited? Have you written the great American thriller? If so, try this spell to sell.

Tools:
Pen and paper
Something that represents what you want to sell
Any oil or incense whose scent makes you feel optimistic
3 candles: red, gold, and violet
When: Three consecutive nights, beginning with the full moon

The item you choose to represent what you want to sell is especially important in this spell. If, for instance, you're a realtor and are trying to sell a particular house or property, then you might choose a little house or a hotel from a Monopoly game to represent the property. If you want to sell a manuscript or screenplay, then perhaps a book or a DVD can serve as a symbol. On a piece of paper, write your desire in the present tense. "My screenplay sells quickly" or "The Smith house sells quickly." Slip this under the item that symbolizes your desire.

Light the oil or incense. As you light the red candle, say your desire out loud three times. The red brings energy into your desire. Let the candle and the incense burn out naturally. Leave the vestiges of the red candle on your altar or wherever you do the spell.

On the second night, repeat this ritual but light the gold candle. It represents your desire for success. Let the candle and incense burn out and leave the spent gold candle next to the red one. On the third night, light the purple candle. The purple symbolizes your highest good. When it burns out, toss out all three candles, releasing your desire.

Another Spell to Sell a Creative Product

This spell comes from June, Lady Ciaran, to her coven.

Tools:
Basil
Cinnamon
A yellow taper candle (pink will do, but yellow is best)
Ballpoint pen
When: During the waxing moon (new moon to first quarter)

Using the pen, inscribe the name of your book, with arrows pointing to it (up and down) into the candle. Figure out your lucky book number. To do this, take the number of pages in your book and add the digits together. If, for example, your book has 256 pages, then add 2 + 5 + 6. The outcome is your lucky book number. Light the candle and chant the following as many times as your lucky book number.

My book/product, [name of book/product], is the one I'm sending off.
I've worked and slaved over it. Please let my talent be enough.
Please let the publisher/agent read/use/watch it and love it.
By the power of this candle I have lit,
So Mote It Be!

Spells for Business

The quality of your professional life is intimately connected with your beliefs about prosperity and success. If you feel unworthy, this will be reflected in your pocketbook and in your work. If, on the other hand, you believe you're deserving—of a raise, a promotion, better working conditions—this will also be reflected in your life.

Where Do You Stand?

In the following brainstorming activity, you're going to take inventory of your professional life—the work you do, your bosses and the people who have power over you, your coworkers or employees, or your personal professional circumstances if you're self-employed.

If you work for someone else:

1. Describe the work that you do, using specific details.
2. Is your work satisfying? Why or why not?
3. Do you get along with your boss?
4. Do you get along with your coworkers?
5. Are you passionate about your work?
6. What would you change about your work if you could?
7. Do you have moral or ethical objections to the work you do?
8. Do you feel you're paid fairly for what you do?

9. What are your professional goals for the next year? The next five years?
10. Do you have regrets about the professional path you've chosen?
11. Have you gotten regular promotions and raises? If not, why?
12. Is your work life filled with power struggles? If so, explain.

If you are self-employed:

1. What type of service or product do you provide?
2. Do you have employees? If so, how many?
3. Do you like most of your employees? Do they do a good job? If not, explain.
4. What would you like to change about your business and why?
5. Do you consider yourself a fair boss?
6. Are you earning enough for what you do?
7. What are your professional goals for the next year? The next five years?
8. If you could choose to do anything you wanted, what would it be? Why?
9. Are you passionate about what you do?
10. If your passions lie elsewhere, can you imagine earning your living at it?

If your answers to the above questions are primarily positive, then you're probably exactly where you want to be in life right now. If the answers are predominantly negative, keep them in mind as you read the chapter.

Spells and Goals

Setting goals is intrinsic to professional achievement. The goals don't have to be set in stone, but it's important to have a bigger picture in mind concerning what you would like to accomplish professionally. Whether you want to change professions or jobs, or to simply move ahead in the profession or job you presently have, setting goals helps you clarify what you want. Once you know what you're after, it's easier to use the proper spells.

Write down your goals for three specific periods of time—you can select the time divisions that work for you. If you're an impatient person, make the increments small—a few days, six weeks—so that you can see your progress quickly. If you've got the patience of a saint, you can extend the increments out over a larger chunk of time.

A Spell for Clarification

This spell is intended to clarify a goal that you have. Quite often, we think we want one thing only to find later that what we wanted was something else entirely. So before you get to that "later on" point, do this simple spell for clarification.

Tools:
A few drops of cedar oil
Pen and paper
When: As you feel the need

Put the drops of cedar oil in your burner and light it. As the scent suffuses the air, write down your goal. Keep it simple. Now shut your eyes and sit quietly for a few moments with your goal in mind. Imagine that you have achieved this goal. How does it feel? Are you comfortable with it? How do your family and friends act toward you? What is your life like now that you have attained what you wanted?

The more vivid and detailed your imaginings, the greater benefit you derive from this visualization. Do this as long as you can keep imagining vividly, then stop. Now read your goal again. Is it what you really want? If not, rewrite it. You may find that you merely need to fine-tune what you've written.

If you rewrite your goal, let it sit for a day or two before you look at it again. Then ask yourself if it feels right. Chances are, it will.

Make a Business Charm

A charm is basically the Western equivalent of a shaman's medicine bundle. It should be small enough to carry with you, yet large enough to accommodate the objects you put inside.

Tools:
Objects that represent your desire (see directions)

The bundle for a charm for business power should be made of cotton or silk, and the color should represent the chakra you use most frequently in your work. If you do a lot of talking in your job, then blue might be the best color for the bag because blue represents the throat chakra, the center of your expression. If your job entails counseling, then the cloth might be a mixture of blue for expression and green to represent the compassion of the heart chakra. (If you're unsure about which color to use, consult the color list in Chapter 4.)

Keep the number of objects in your bundle to a minimum, and be sure the items symbolize something important to you. You can also put slips of paper with your desires or needs written on them in your bundle. From time to time, cleanse the items in your bundle by washing them in sea salt and charging them in the sun. If they can't be washed, simply set them outside in the sun for a few minutes. As your charm works its magick on particular projects or issues, consider replacing the items with other objects.

New Ventures

A new job, a new profession, a new lease on your professional life—all of these things fall in this category. Nothing can be as frightening as the prospect of starting something new. We worry about whether we should give it a whirl. We worry about whether we're young enough, experienced enough, or talented enough to make a go of it. We worry because we've been conditioned to worry, to berate ourselves, to assume we don't have what it takes. That's not true—but sometimes you *do* need a little help to get you started.

A young writer once wrote a book, didn't think it was good enough to be published, and tossed it in the garbage. His wife retrieved the manuscript and it was not only published, it became a bestseller and a movie. The author? Stephen King. The book? *Carrie.*

Back in the early 1980s, a young woman had an idea about color and skin tones. But she didn't know how to put it together. On a plane trip, she happened to sit next to a young man and told him her idea. He became second in command, she became the CEO, and the company was called Color Me Beautiful. Sometimes, it takes another person—or a little magick—to recognize your genius and help you organize it.

A Spell to Recognize Your Genius

This spell is intended to attract the individual who recognizes your genius and helps you pull together your vision of what might be, whatever that vision is.

Tools:
Seeds for a plant that has round leaves or purple flowers
Ceramic pot
Potting soil
When: Thursday during a waxing moon

Fill your ceramic pot with potting soil and place nine seeds at various points in the soil. As you plant the seeds, say aloud:

As I plant these seeds
I draw to me
The one who sees
What I can be.
So mote it be.

Once the seeds begin to sprout, the person who recognizes your genius should appear in your life. Until that happens, keep the plant in the northern section of your home—the place for career. Or, if that isn't possible, locate the wall or section of your house that is directly opposite your front door. If you have a particular room in your house where you do most of your work, the pot could also go in there, along the wall opposite the door or along the northern wall.

A Spell to Enhance Magnetism

This spell helps on that first day in a new job, with a new boss, new coworkers, new ventures, and new professional situations.

> *Tools:*
> A red candle
> A violet candle
> A quartz crystal
> Your favorite oil
> *When:* During the waxing moon

This spell enhances your aura and fills it with magnetism that attracts what you need. It also protects you from what you don't need. The quartz crystal amplifies the magnetism. Light your burner and as the scent suffuses the air, inhale deeply, and light the red candle. Say aloud:

> *The magnetism of this red flame*
> *Enters me by name,*
> *[say your name]*
> *So mote it be.*

Light the violet candle and say:

> *The protection of this violet flame*
> *Enters me by name*

[say your name]
So mote it be.

Let the candles burn out naturally. Bury them in your yard or in a flowerpot, so the power stays with you always.

So Much to Do, So Little Time

No matter how hard you work, you never seem to get caught up. If stress and frustration are getting you down, this spell offers a welcome respite from workplace demands.

Tools:
Lavender incense
An incense burner
A light blue candle
A candleholder
Matches or a lighter
A bathtub
Essential oil of vanilla
4 good-sized chunks of amethyst
When: Any time

Cast a Circle around your bathroom. Fit the incense and candle into their respective holders, then light both. Fill the bathtub with pleasantly hot water. Add a little essential oil of vanilla to the bathwater.

Wash the amethysts with mild soap and water, then set one on each corner of the bathtub. Climb into the tub and make yourself comfy. Feel the amethysts drawing off your stress and neutralizing it. Feel your frustrations and anxieties dissolving into the bathwater. The trick is not to think about anything outside the walls of the bathroom.

When you worry about the past or future, you block receptivity to new ideas and guidance that could help you resolve problems. If a troublesome thought pops into your mind, send it into the water or give it to the amethysts. Soak for as long as you like until you feel calm, rested, and confident that all is well.

When your peace of mind is restored, get out of the tub. As the water drains away, visualize your cares flowing away with it. Pick up the amethysts and thank them. Then wash them with clean water (not the bathwater) and mild soap and pat them dry. Extinguish the candle and incense, or allow them to burn down in a safe place. Open the Circle and emerge renewed.

A Spell to Beat Out the Competition

The competition's trying to move into your territory or edge you out of the picture. But you have a secret weapon: magick. This spell lets you rise above the rest of the pack and keeps infringers from gaining a foothold.

Tools:
Polymer clay
A large needle
Jewelry elastic
A nonstick baking tray
When: On a Tuesday, or when the sun or moon is in Aries

Have you ever seen animals defend their territory? They usually attack with teeth and claws. This spell takes its cue from them. You're going to fabricate "teeth" and "claws" from polymer clay to draw on the same symbolism.

Select white or ivory clay to simulate the real thing, or another color if you prefer (who knows what color dragon's teeth are?). Follow the directions on the package of clay to form lots of pointy teeth and claws, each about an inch or two in length. With the needle, pierce each one at the thicker end, making a hole large enough so the jewelry elastic will fit through it. Arrange the teeth and claws on the baking tray, making sure they don't touch each other. Bake according to instructions on the package.

Cut a piece of jewelry elastic long enough to go over your head. When the teeth and claws have cooked and cooled, string them onto jewelry elastic to make a necklace. Tie the elastic in a knot at the back. Wear this warrior's necklace to bolster your own courage, so you can scare off the competition and defend what's yours.

A Spell to Birth a New Project

You're having a hard time getting a project off the ground. Delays, deterrents, and disappointments keep interfering with your progress. This spell "fertilizes" your idea and helps you bring your venture to fruition. The custom of painting eggs at Easter originated with the early festival of Ostara, which is held on the Spring Equinox. Eggs are symbols of birth, life, and fertility, and Ostara celebrates the Earth's renewal after the long, cold winter.

Tools:
A raw egg
A straight pin or needle
A bowl
Acrylic or watercolor paints
A small paintbrush
Water
When: On the Spring Equinox, or on the new moon

Carefully poke a hole in each end of the egg with a pin. Holding the egg above the bowl, place your mouth over one hole and gently blow the contents of the egg out through the other hole. When you've finished, rinse out the eggshell and let it dry.

Paint symbols and images on the eggshell that represent your project, as well as your objectives. Make sure everything you include has positive connotations for you. While you work, visualize your project moving forward and receiving the support and acclaim you seek. See your goals coming to fruition, your success assured.

When you've finished decorating your egg, display it in a place where you'll see it often. Each time you look at it, you'll be reminded of your goal and your intention to succeed.

A Spell to Get a Raise or Promotion

Do this spell only if you're convinced that you're worthy of a raise or a promotion. Otherwise, you're just saying words. The bill you use to represent your raise can be of any denomination. It's merely a symbol.

Tools:
2 gold candles
$20 bill that represents your raise
Sprig of sage
Pen and paper
When: During the waxing moon, preferably on a Thursday night

Jot down what you would like your raise to be. Phrase it in the present tense and add "or better" at the end of it. Your statement might read: "I get a $5,000 raise or better." If you're doing this for a job promotion, jot it down in the same format.

Set the piece of paper and the bill between the gold candles. Light the sprig of sage. As you light the candles, say aloud:

Element of fire,
Hear my desire,
A raise/promotion is due to me,
[state what you want] or better,
Make it so to the letter.

Once you feel the rightness of what you're saying, once it resonates inside of you, then burn the piece of paper on which you wrote what you wanted, thus releasing the desire. Pinch out the flames and toss out the candles and the ashes of the sage.

Power Symbols

An object is merely an object until it has, for lack of a better word, soul. That soul comes from the person who owns it, touches it, or takes care of it, and in doing so, imbues that thing with the uniqueness of who he or she is. Objects absorb and reflect our energy, just by being in the same space that we inhabit. If we're passionate about something, that energy is heightened. It lingers, without any effort on our part. But when we consciously imbue an object with our passion, intent, and desires, then the object becomes extremely powerful. If you need a bit of power on your side to help you gain the upper hand in a business situation—or any situation—make sure that the objects around you are there for a purpose and not just for decoration.

A Spell for the Frequent Business Flyer

If you travel frequently on business, this spell can save you time, aggravation, and stress. Do this spell several hours before you leave for the airport.

Tools:
Several drops of amber or sandalwood oil
A violet or purple candle
Sprig of sage
Pen and paper
When: As needed

On a sheet of paper, write: *My trip unfolds smoothly. I arrive safely and on time at my destination.* Set the paper next to the candle. Light the burner for the amber or sandalwood oil, then light the sage. Now light your candle and read what you've written out loud. Read it again silently and envision yourself at your destination, on time, with your bags, refreshed and at peace.

Read what you've written aloud once more, then burn it, releasing your desire. Blow or pinch out the candles and toss them out with the sage. Blow out the candle in the burner and give thanks that you are in a position to travel.

Mitigating Negative Situations

Most of us have bad days now and then at work. Occasionally, however, a bad day collapses into a really negative situation. Then it's more difficult to get back on the right track because it seems we're bogged down by negativity.

✳ **Wiccan Wonderings: How do you find the right amulet for business power?**

An amulet isn't something you can look for. It comes to you, it appears, it falls off a shelf at your feet. It can be any object that resonates with you. The actual object matters less than the sentiment you attach to it. It simply must be something that speaks to you, and when you first see it, you know it's yours. This applies to amulets for business, love, travel, or anything else. In situations like this, the longer you dwell on what went wrong, the worse it looks and the more negative and bleak your outlook becomes. It's one of those self-perpetuating cycles. To break the cycle and mitigate the negative situation, the first thing you have to do is step back and detach emotionally from whatever has happened. Remember that your point of power resides in the moment. You can't change what has happened, but you can alter your perspective about it and that, in turn, can soften the impact.

A Spell to Release Negativity

If the situation is pressing, you can do this spell at any time. But any spell to release or cleanse is most powerful during the waning moon.

Tools:
A white candle
A bay leaf

White flowers, preferably carnations
When: During the waning moon

Place the bay leaf next to your vase of flowers and light your candle. Say aloud:

I now release [name the situation]
and create new, positive energy to carry me forward.
I trust this is for my highest good
and affirm my commitment to this new path.
I say so mote it be.

Let the candles burn out on their own. Toss out the bay leaf with the flowers when they die.

A Point of Power Spell

With this spell, you're affirming that your point of power is in the present. The moment is your launching pad for the rest of your life. You can do this spell in conjunction with the previous spell or you can do it alone, for virtually any situation or issue.

Tools:
Ginger
Potted plant with yellow flowers
A green candle
A purple candle
When: Thursday or Friday during a waxing moon

With this spell, you're affirming in your own mind that your point of power is, indeed, in the present. Put the ginger between each of the candles and the plant behind the ginger. As you light the candles, say aloud:

My point of power,
like this plant that flowers,
some way, somehow
lies in the now.

Pinch out the candles when you're finished and toss out the ginger. Put the potted plant into the soil where you can see it. If it's not possible to plant it outside, then transplant it into a larger pot and put it in a window where you can see it.

A Spell to Protect Your Job

If your job is on the line, for reasons that may or may not be your fault, you're likely stressed out. Instead of worrying, which will only make matters worse, use your time and energy more productively by casting this spell.

Tools:
4 white stones
Black paint or a black felt-tip marker with permanent ink
When: Any time

Collect four white stones. Wash the stones with mild soap and water. Allow them to dry in the sun. With the black paint or marker, draw a pentagram (a five-pointed star with a circle around it) on each stone. Pentagrams are ancient magick symbols of protection and security.

Put one stone on the floor in each corner of your cubicle, office, or work area to stabilize your position. As you set each stone in place, say or think this affirmation: "My job here is safe and secure, and all is well."

Chapter 13

Spells for Your Home

Your home mirrors your feelings about where you live and whatever you've experienced while living in the house. This sounds obvious, until you're confronted with the profundity of what it actually means. Nowhere is the significance more apparent than when you see the reflections in other people's homes.

For most of us, our impressions about a house are probably formed the moment we walk in the front door. We immediately sense whether the place is friendly or hostile, chaotic or organized, formal or casual. We immediately like it or dislike it. Usually, our feelings don't have much to do with the furnishings or the color of the rugs, and they might not even be related to the layout of the rooms. We're reacting, instead, to a general overall impression, a feeling tone.

A Home's Unique Personality

In homes that aren't brand new, the feeling tone is something that has built up over a period of months or years. If the people who live in the house are predominately happy, we feel it. If tragedies have happened in the house, we feel that, too. Houses, like people, carry emotional baggage. If you've ever gone house-hunting, you've probably noticed the feelings you pick up when you walk inside a house and through its rooms. It's almost as if the walls hold secrets, the floors whisper tales, and the porches laugh or weep.

Even new houses have a certain feeling tone. You can sense that everyone from the architects to the tradespeople has left his or her imprint on the rooms. Houses, apartments, duplexes—all of them speak to us. Even hotels have voices. The Overlook Hotel in Stephen King's classic *The Shining* has absorbed decades of emotions from the guests who have stayed there, and that emotional residue has taken on a life of its own. In a sense, that hotel is very much alive.

The same is true in Shirley Jackson's book *The Haunting of Hill House*, in Richard Matheson's novel *A Stir of Echoes*, and in every similar story ever written or filmed. The difference between fiction and life, however, is that the energy that imbues a place isn't always bad. It's often uplifting, buoyant, and optimistic. It might even make us feel on top of the world as soon as we cross the threshold.

What is the feeling tone of the place where you live? Use the following "Brainstorming" exercise to find out:

1. Describe your home.
2. Describe how you feel about your home.
3. What would you change about where you live, and why?
4. Describe how you feel most of the time when you're at home.
5. Is your home spacious enough to accommodate everyone who lives in it comfortably?
6. Are the rooms cluttered?
7. Which areas or items in your home don't work or need attention? Think about your attic, basement, roof, doors, floors, walls, carpets, sinks and faucets, electrical outlets, and so on.
8. How do most people react to visiting your home?
9. Do you like your neighborhood? Why or why not?
10. Describe your dream house.
11. Why did you rent/lease/buy this place?
12. Overall, how would you describe your experiences in this house? Have you been predominantly happy, sad, or indifferent?

Analyzing Your Home

Question 7 is especially important because it helps identify possible challenges and problems in your life right now. Look at the various listings as a metaphor. Let's say your garage door is stuck. It won't go up. If we look at the metaphor for what a garage door represents, perhaps you have trouble admitting new people and experiences into your life. Maybe you feel trapped. Maybe you don't know how to open a door to opportunity.

The answers to 8 and 12 might be similar. If your experiences in your home are predominately positive, that is probably what other people will feel. The reverse is also true. This doesn't mean that the feeling tones of a place are confined to either/or, good or bad, black or white. Quite often, we live in shades of gray. We walk the middle. We don't experience extremes. Our homes also absorb that.

With spells, you can protect, energize, and calm your home. You can cleanse it of negative energy, boost its positive energy, ward off potential enemies or problems, and create atmospheres of success and happiness within its walls. You can make your home easier to sell and you can cast spells to find the home of your dreams. In short, you can do for your home and living space what you do for yourself. The same rules apply. It's all about belief, intent, and desire.

A Spell to Get Rid of Negative Energy

This ritual originates with Native Americans and is a popular method for cleansing just about anything. When burned, sage is a sweet-smelling herb. Some types smell like burning marijuana; others smell of summer in the great outdoors. But the scent of the sage is less important than the cleansing properties of the sage itself. During the waning moon is the ideal time for this spell because you're getting rid of something. You're purging. You're doing the equivalent of a *limpieza*, or cleansing, in Santería.

Tools:
Sage, the herb (basil can be used as an alternative)
When: During the waning moon

To cleanse a room, simply pass the smoke of the burning sage over the walls, into the corners, in the closets, and in any nooks and crannies where shadows—and energy—gather. Pass the smoke along the frames of the doors and windows. Let it eddy across the floor. This simple process is vital whenever something tragic, negative, or emotionally wrenching has happened. It's also beneficial if someone in your home is physically ill or feeling out of sorts. You don't have to say anything or engage in any ritual. Simply hold the intent in your mind that you are cleaning the area of negative energy.

A sage wand is ideal for smudging. It doesn't have to be relit, it's easy to carry, and when you're finished, you simply stub out the burning end so that it can be used again.

A Spell to Invite Greater Happiness Into Your Home

Inviting happiness into your home shouldn't be confined to a particular time of day or night, or even to any phase of the moon. Before you run out for plants and oils, however, you should smudge your home to clear out any negative energy (see previous spell).

Tools:
Several round-leaf houseplants
Violet- or lavender-scented incense or oil
Vase of freshly cut flowers
When: Any time

Select your houseplants with care. Round-leaf plants are friendlier symbolically than, say, cacti or any plants with pointed leaves. Jade plants are excellent choices. They do well indoors, especially if near a window, have gently rounded leaves, and represent wealth, prosperity, and happiness.

Place your houseplants with the same care with which you selected them. Usually, every room has several "power spots" where plants seem to flourish. Quite often, the family pet will snooze in or near power spots. Or you may sense them on your own. As you place your houseplants, request that they bring happiness into your home.

Freshly cut flowers enhance the energy in any home. Select flowers that are brilliantly colored or that seize your attention.

> ✴ **Wiccan Wonderings: How can you boost a home's positive energy?**
> We often know instinctively when our homes need an infusion of energy. It's mostly common sense. We paint things a different color, rearrange or buy new furniture, clear clutter, or repair what doesn't work. All of these things shift energy. You can also smudge the rooms, then burn a white scented candle in each room, allowing them to burn out naturally. Follow this with a brief meditation requesting that harmony and happiness enter the house.

You don't have to have incense or oils burning constantly in your home to invite happiness inside. You might simply light one or the other as you're placing the plants in your house and arranging the fresh flowers.

Making these small gestures toward inviting happiness into your home—and thus, into your life—might inspire you to go even further. Do any of the rooms need to be painted? Are blinds broken or curtains torn? Maybe it's time for a general facelift.

The People and Pets at Home

The people and pets who share your living space contribute to the overall feeling texture of your home. If you have a roommate or someone else in your home with whom you don't get along or who is mostly negative, then you need to take measures to rid the rooms of that negativity. This may call for a sage smudging at regular intervals: Do so once a week for a month, then once a month after that. Other remedial adjustments might also be in order. You can include a piece of onyx or burn a black candle in or near the person's room to absorb the negative energy. If you burn a black candle, let it burn all the way down, then toss it out. You don't have to throw out the onyx; just bathe it in sea water (or water with some sea salt in it if you don't live near an ocean) and then set it in the sun for a few minutes to charge it.

If you have a pet who is hostile toward you or other people, you might try a little feng shui magick. Locate the family area of your home. This area lies in the eastern part of the house or, in Western feng shui, the farthest left-hand side of your house when you stand inside your front door. Add a tabletop fountain to the family area, a couple of jade plants, and something black. And, of course, don't forget to give your pet plenty of love.

If you have children, the best area in feng shui lies in the western part of the house or, if you're standing in the front door, directly opposite the family area. If your kids are hostile or angry, use anything yellow in that area—flowers (with round leaves), curtains, linen, quilts, whatever feels right. Symbols for children and creativity are also good here, as are music, bells, and lights.

Once the negativity in the children's area is purged, put a white crystal or white flowers somewhere in the room. It helps to balance emotions.

Selling Your Home Quickly

Few things are more frustrating than putting your house on the market and then having it sit there, month after excruciating month, with no progress. There are always dozens of rational excuses for why a house hasn't sold—the wrong time of year, rising interest rates, the house needs work, the neighborhood isn't close enough to schools. But it only takes one person to buy your home, and a little help from the universe doesn't hurt!

If you're trying to sell your home and could use a boost, begin with a smudging, using sage. Start in the room that is visible as you step in the front door, then smudge in each of the four directions, followed by the doorways, baseboards, windows, closets, and everything else. Repeat this process in every room, then proceed to the next spell.

✳ **Wiccan Wonderings: What should you do when your house won't sell?**
To sell your home, you must be ready to release it and let go emotionally. Until you can imagine yourself living elsewhere without regrets, no spell in the universe will help. Make peace with your home, expressing your gratitude toward it for having sheltered and protected you. This might feel odd, but do it anyway. Spend a few minutes in each room, remembering good experiences and smudging each room as you walk through. Then watch how things unfold.

A Spell to Sell

Tools:
A gold candle
A red candle
Your favorite oil
When: During a waning moon

Before you even list your house with a realtor or put out that "for sale" sign, light your oil burner with your favorite oil inside. Place a red candle on one side of the burner and a gold on the otherside. As you light each one, say:

My house sells quickly
For at least [state the price you want].
Make it so.

Repeat this throughout the waning moon period. Allow the candles to burn out naturally.

A Spell to Find a Home

Tools:
Paper, pen, glue, scissors, poster board
When: During the full moon

You can either sketch the house you're looking for or find pictures or photographs that depict the house and create a wish board. A wish board consists of a poster board covered with photos, pictures, sayings, and affirmations that relate to one or several different goals and desires. It's a powerful visualization device, especially when you put the poster somewhere so visible that you can't help but see it.

The idea is to create a visual tool for what you desire. Make it vivid and detailed. Get the rest of the family involved. Kids love doing this sort of thing and often come up with things you didn't think of. The more energy that is poured into the desire, the quicker it will materialize.

A Spell to Protect Your House

A word of caution about this spell. In one sense, it implies a belief in victimization. However, there are times when we feel better knowing that the odds are stacked in our favor, so if you use the spell in that spirit, it can be applied to any number of situations.

Tools:
Cedar oil
Animal totem
When: Whenever you feel the need

The totem you select should be that of an animal with which you feel a kinship and that represents protective power to you. Light your burner and when the scent begins to billow from it, pass the totem through it and say:

Protect this home,
High to low,
Fence to fence,
Door to door,
Light to dense,
Roof to floor.

Moving Into a New Home

Any kind of move entails a monumental shift in energy. You are shifting gears not only in the physical world, but on a metaphysical level as well. Quite often, moves coincide with other major life events and experiences—births, marriages, divorces, death, work transfers, or new jobs. Not only do you have to contend with the physical logistics, but there are psychological adjustments as well. Whether the move is a few miles away or across the country, it can be stressful for everyone involved. Even when a move goes smoothly, you're faced with the daunting task of unpacking your belongings at the other end. Spells can help ease the stress.

A Spell to Ensure a Smooth Move

If at all possible, it's wisest not to move when Mercury is retrograde. When a planet is going retrograde, it means that from our viewpoint here on Earth, it appears to be moving backward through the Zodiac. Since Mercury rules communication and travel, glitches usually show up when the planet is retrograde. Check with an astrologer or on any of the astrology sites on the Web for the periods when Mercury is retrograde.

Tools:
Basil oil or sprig of chamomile
When: Every Friday night for the month before you move

Every Friday night for the month before you move, burn some basil oil or burn a sprig of chamomile. The first promotes harmony and the second blesses a person, place, or thing. As you light both, vividly imagine your move going smoothly and seamlessly, with everything clicking into place and unfolding according to plan.

A Spell to Bless a New Home

Tools:
Sage
Broom
A bottle of wine or apple cider
A loaf of freshly baked bread

Begin by smudging your home with sage to clear away any unwanted energies. Then, use the broom to sweep out the vibrations left behind by the former occupants. When this is done, pour the wine (or cider) and slice the bread. The bread and wine ensure that you will always have enough to eat and drink in your new home. Share this magick meal with all who will live in the home with you and/or any friends who will enjoy visiting you there.

A Magick Garden

For centuries wise men and women have grown flowers and herbs for medicinal, culinary, and magickal purposes. You can, too. Choose from the list below, depending on where you live and which plants you like best. If a garden isn't feasible for your space, plant herbs or flowers in window boxes or flowerpots. Warning: Some favorite plants of protection are poisonous, so if you decide to include them in your garden, make sure they won't be accessible to children or pets. Also, wear gardening gloves while working with these plants.

Tools:
A gardening trowel or shovel
Gardening gloves

Flowerpots (optional)
Potting soil (optional)
As many of the following plants as you wish to include in your
garden: white snapdragons, basil, white peonies, St. John's wort,
foxglove (poisonous), aconite (poisonous), garlic, fennel, white clover, thyme, ferns, poppies, rosemary, yucca, cactus, blessed thistle
When: During the waxing moon, preferably when the moon is
in Taurus

Plant the flowers and herbs you've chosen, according to their particular soil and light requirements. As you work, envision them pro-
viding a protective shield around your residence. Ask the plants to
safeguard you and your home. Care for the plants and they'll continue to care for you.

Parting Thoughts about Home

Become more aware of how you enter and leave your home. Do you
arrive or depart in anger, slamming doors and muttering to yourself? Or
do you arrive and depart with respect for the space itself? Do you take
off your shoes when you enter your house? In Japan, the removal of
shoes is considered respectful.

Whether arriving or departing, you are imbuing the house with
your energy. If the energy is angry, hostile, or sad, then over a period of
time that becomes the dominant energy in the house. If, on the other
hand, the energy is upbeat and happy, that becomes the dominant
energy. When you live with other people, of course, you can't control
how they feel within the house. But at least you can make them more
aware of how they enter and leave.

A home with kids, pets, and live plants is apt to be filled with lively,
upbeat energy. The chi also flows better. Live plants are telling about the
general mood in the house. If they flourish, then the dominant energy is
probably upbeat and positive.

If you work at home, then it's even more important to keep the dominant mood in your house upbeat and positive. Develop awareness of and respect for the place where you live, and your life there will be much more enjoyable.

Chapter 14

Spells for Travel

If you fly commercially at all, you're no doubt familiar with this scenario. You arrive at the airport an hour or more ahead of your flight, check your bags, and half an hour later find out the flight is going to be delayed several hours—or worse, canceled. Maybe you're fortunate and your flight leaves on time, but every seat is filled and you're crammed in a window seat, next to someone who coughs constantly during the flight or has a crying baby. To make things worse, the guy in front of you lowers the back of his seat all the way down, so that your knees are nearly crammed under your chin.

Welcome to air travel in the twenty-first century. Even if you arrive at your destination on time, the physical discomforts of air travel are often considerable and they, in turn, create emotional turmoil. Is there any way to mitigate the effects?

Ritual to Extend Your Energy Field for Travel

To counter space constraints on a flight, your best bet is to extend your aura. People generally sense each other's boundaries and if your energy extends several feet from your body, it's less likely that someone will violate your personal space.

When: As needed

Ten or fifteen minutes before you board your flight, sit with your feet flat on the floor and focus on the tips of your shoes. Stare until your vision begins to blur, then imagine yourself in a cocoon of white light.

The cocoon should encompass all of you, from the tips of your toes to the top of your head. At first the cocoon may be small, extending a few inches from your body. Imagine the cocoon expanding, filling with even more light. Color the light if you want—any color except black will work. Imagine the cocoon of light expanding until it stretches several feet from your body in all directions.

When you feel the energy has expanded to where you want it, silently repeat:

I am safe, protected, and comfortable throughout my flight.

Repeat this several times. Then tell yourself that every time you repeat this phrase, your energy field will automatically expand so that it stretches at least two or three feet from your body.

During your flight, repeat the phrase whenever you feel the need. If you do this when you're jammed in a window or middle seat, the person next to you is going to feel it. The person may shift his body away from yours. If you maintain the cocoon at several feet, the person may even get up and move to another seat—if there are any.

Visualization to Deal with the Person in Front of You

If you've got someone reclining in front of you, try this visualization.

When: As needed

The first thing to do when you feel cramped by the person in front of you is calm yourself. Resist the urge to jackknife your legs against the seat. Maintain your extended aura. Shut your eyes and focus on your heart. Visualize waves of soft, pale light pouring from your heart's energy center. Extend the waves until they spill over the seat in front of you. Imagine the waves of light surrounding the person in front of you. When you feel reasonably sure that the light surrounds the person, silently request that he put his seat up.

Repeat your request several times. If this doesn't work, extend the light even farther. Your success is dependent on how vividly you can imagine the light. A word of caution about the light: sometimes it makes the other person fall asleep.

Visualization to Calm a Crying Baby

Infants are sensitive to the change in atmospheric pressure on a plane, and it's likely that crying may help them clear their ears. If you're seated next to or near a crying infant, the surest way to ease the child's misery—and thus your own—is to work from the heart energy center.

Once again, imagine light pouring from your heart center. It can be any pastel color. Let the light surround the child, cradling it. When you feel the child within the light, rock the light gently, as though you were holding the child in your arms. Whisper to the child in your mind. Keep this up for several moments even after the child stops crying.

A Spell for Traveling During the Waxing Moon

If you're going to be traveling when the moon is waxing, this spell should be done the day before you leave. It's more powerful if you do it at night, but it can be done during the day as well.

Tools:
A white candle
Rosemary, oil or herb
When: As needed, within twenty-four hours before your departure

Light the rosemary. As you light the white candle, say:

In the light of the growing moon,
I am protected and blessed in my journey,
And arrive at my destination soon.

Fear of Flying Spell

If the idea of soaring eight miles above the Earth in a metal cylinder makes you feel weak in your knees, you're not alone. And what about all those terrorist stories you keep hearing? What can you do to calm your fears of flying? One way is to enlist the aid of the air spirits, known as sylphs.

Tools:
Clove incense
An incense burner
Matches or a lighter
A fan made of feathers (or a single large feather)
White carnation petals
A container in which to carry the carnation petals
When: On a Wednesday or Thursday, at least a day before your trip

If possible, perform this spell outside. Collect the ingredients needed for this spell. Cast a Circle around the place where you'll perform your spell. Fit the incense into its burner and light it. Waft the smoke toward you with the fan (or use the feather and your hand to guide the smoke toward you). Turn around, allowing the smoke to touch all sides of your body. Tap both shoulders with the fan, then tap your body at the places where the seven main charkas or energy centers are located, starting at the crown chakra and ending at the root chakra.

Invite the sylphs to join you. Sylphs are nature spirits who serve as ambassadors of the element of air. You may see faint flickering lights or feel a shift in the air around you as they come to answer your call. They might even appear to you as tiny Tinkerbell-like beings.

Request their assistance on your trip. Express your concerns and explain what you would like them to do for you. Speak to them with courtesy and respect, as you would to a human being from whom you sought aid. Tell them you've brought a gift to thank them in advance for helping you. Open the container and scatter the carnation petals in the wind. You may notice that the wind picks up or changes direction as the sylphs accept your offering.

If you wish, take the fan or feather with you when you fly, to remind you that you are protected by the spirits of the air.

A Spell for Traveling During the Waning Moon

The waning moon is a time of decrease, so you need a bit of a boost when traveling under this moon phase. The white flower you use in this spell should be broken off just below the bud, so the petals float on the surface of the water. Any kind of white flower can be used.

Tools:
A white candle
A gold candle
White flower in a bowl of water
When: As needed, or twenty-four hours before your departure

As you light the candles, imagine that any negativity associated with your trip is absorbed by the flower. Then say aloud:

As time does tell,
My journey goes well.
So mote it be.

Visualization to Create Space in Your Head

This visualization technique works for claustrophobia, but also mitigates fear, near-panic, anxiety, and high emotions.

When: As needed

Center yourself with a couple of deep breaths, then create a mental image of a wide-open space—the beach, the ocean, a field, a park, or even an open road. If you imagine somewhere that has personal significance to you, the visualization will be more vivid. When, for instance, you imagine your favorite beach, you can almost feel the hot sand against your bare feet, smell the scent of salt in the air, see the blue perfection of the water, and hear gulls screeching through the sunlight. The more personal the image, the better it works.

The tricky part is holding the image long enough to convince your body and emotions that the crisis has passed. But with practice, nearly anyone can do it.

A Spell for Smooth Sailing

This spell is great for travel in general, but is especially good for long-distance air travel, foreign or domestic.

Tools:
A white candle
Your favorite herb or aromatic oil
Object that represents your trip
When: Twenty-four hours before your departure

The day before your departure, light your herb or burner. As the scent permeates the air, light the candle and say aloud:

By this flame's bright light
My trip to [name destination]

Unfolds smoothly, on time, without blight.
Make it so.

Pass the object through the smoke of the herb or oil, then snuff out the candle and toss it out.

Travel Spell for Cats

Most cats hate to travel. They don't like confinement, the motion makes them feel insecure, and they get anxious when taken out of their familiar environments. This spell eases your cat's anxiety and makes the trip more pleasant for both of you.

> *Tools:*
> Homeopathic remedy Cocculus Indicus 30c
> Bach Flower Rescue Remedy (see following sidebar)
> A piece of amethyst
> A spray bottle
> Water
> Lavender essential oil
> A blue blanket, towel, or pad
> The largest cage that will fit in your car
> *When:* An hour before you start your trip

About an hour before you start your trip, put one tiny Cocculus Indicus pill in your cat's mouth and make sure she swallows it. (If you prefer, you can dissolve the pill in water, then give her the water with an eyedropper.) Then put a drop of Rescue Remedy on her nose (she'll lick it off).

Place the amethyst in the bottle and fill it with water. Add a few drops of essential oil and shake the bottle three times to charge it. Mist the inside of your car with the fragrant water. Repeat this periodically throughout the trip.

Lay the blanket, towel, or pad in the bottom of the cat's cage. Gently place the cat in the cage and, if possible, position the cage so your cat will be able to see you while you're traveling. Send calm, loving vibrations from your heart center to your cat. Talk to her in a quiet, soothing voice. If you wish, play soft music while you're driving. If the trip will take more than one day, repeat the same procedure each morning before you start. (Practical tip: Get a collar for your cat with a name tag that includes your name, address, and phone number on it. Label the cage with the same information.)

Bach Flower Rescue Remedy

You can purchase Bach Flower Rescue Remedy and other homeopathic remedies in most health food stores. Flower remedies can also be ordered from the Flower Essence Society, online at www.flowersociety.org. Rescue Remedy and other Bach flower essences can be ordered online from www.bachflower.com.

A Spell to Manifest a Trip You Desire

Is there someplace you've always wanted to go? Don't worry about how you'll get the money or time for the trip—just do your magick and let the universe handle the arrangements.

Tools:
A large sheet of heavy paper or cardboard
Colored markers or pens
Magazine photos of places you want to go
Maps
Other symbols that represent travel to you
Glue
Sandalwood incense
When: During the waxing moon, preferably on a Thursday

Cut out pictures from magazines and travel catalogs of a place you'd like to visit. Gather maps, brochures, and other information about this place. Collect symbols and images that represent travel to you—a toy airplane, a tiny boat, a hotel from a Monopoly game, seashells, and anything that relates to the trip you're planning.

After you've gathered as many images as you feel you need, draw a circle on the piece of paper or cardboard large enough that you can stand within it. Glue all the symbols you've collected inside the circle. Use the colored markers to draw additional pictures and/or write words that describe your intentions, such as the names of the places you plan to visit or affirmations stating your desires.

When your wish board is finished, light the incense. Stand in the middle of the board and envision yourself journeying to the place(s) you've chosen. Make your visualization as clear and vivid as possible. Try to intuit the mood of the place, the sights, sounds, and smells. Enjoy yourself. Remain in the circle, imagining your journey, until the incense finishes burning.

Other Types of Travel

So far, we've concentrated on air travel. But, depending on where you're going and who you're with, travel by car can also be stressful. Any parent who travels by car with young children knows that it can be stressful. *Are we there yet? I have to go to the bathroom. I'm bored.* Writer Nancy Pickard, however, had a more specific challenge. When her son was very young, he used to get car sick. She was reading Louise Hay at the time, and Hay said that the probable emotional cause of motion sickness was a fear of being trapped, of not being in control. Instead of trying to reason with her son about why he shouldn't feel trapped or afraid in the car, she came up with another solution. Every time her son started to feel sick in the car, she would start singing, "I am in control." Her son would start singing it, too, and pretty soon the motion sickness passed. A playful approach to fear or problems often dissolves the underlying emotion before it can take root and grow.

※ **Wiccan Wonderings: What should I do to prepare for a road trip?**

Before you pull out of your driveway, take sixty seconds to imagine surrounding your car with light. White light is probably the best because it's a symbol for protection, but pastels work, too. Avoid black and brilliant colors. Imagine the light as a rubbery cocoon. Trust that you will glide along inside your cocoon through traffic both thick and sparse.

A skeptic might say that singing *I am in control* while a child is about to vomit in your back seat doesn't change anything. That same skeptic would probably also say that affirmations, visualizations, and spells are just spit in the wind. Doubt is easy—maybe one of the easiest things any of us do. It's much tougher to try something that contradicts your beliefs about what is possible just to see what happens.

Quite often, the best time to take the leap is when you travel by car: a long road trip or a trip to the grocery store or to Little League—the where is less important than the trying. So start small. The next time you're circling a parking lot in search of a parking space, create the space in your head. See the parking space, see yourself pulling into it, trust that it'll happen. This type of manifestation is probably one of the simplest to do, if your desire is strong enough. Try it yourself.

Your Traveling Magick Kit

Kids operate under the wisdom of taking a blanket or toy with them when they travel. These objects help them acclimate to a new place because they're familiar and comforting. Your traveling magick kit is meant to fill the same function.

Here are some suggestions about what to include in your kit:

1. Your favorite stone
2. A couple of sticks of your favorite incense
3. A perfume whose scent puts you in a calm, meditative state
4. A small candle

5. A travel-size, unopened container of sea salt
6. A journal to record dreams, experiences, random thoughts

You can even include some other small, personal item that has special significance to you. Then, whenever you're stuck in traffic, or in some other stressful travel situation, simply touching the item will help calm you down. Your magick tools might vary from trip to trip. But you should probably have at least one object that's a staple.

Make a Travel Charm

The charm you use when you travel should contain fewer items than charm bags you use at home. It's a good idea to carry it close to your body. There should be at least one item inside that, when you touch it, communicates a strong sense of safety and protection.

Chapter 15

Where to Go from Here

Now that you've got a sense of how magick works and a hundred-plus spells in your repertoire, it's time to think about taking your craft to the next level. For some, that means practicing with other Witches. The ever-expanding circle of Wiccans and Witches worldwide provides opportunities to express your beliefs in a supportive community and to align your abilities with those of others to bring about a better world for everyone. This chapter will help you decide whether to seek a group to interact with, and if so, how to find the right group.

Covens

The word *coven* originated from the Latin term *coventus,* meaning "assembly" or "agreement." (Covenant comes from the same root.) The term first appeared in Scotland around the 1500s to denote a Witch's meeting or a local group of practicing Witches. However, the word was rarely used until the modern Witchcraft movement became more public and popularized.

In her book *The Spiral Dance,* Starhawk describes a coven as "a Witch's support group, consciousness-raising group, psychic study center, clergy training program, College of Mysteries, surrogate clan, and religious congregation all rolled into one." That about sums it up. In short, a coven is a spiritual family in which each member is committed to the principles of the Craft and to one another.

The traditional coven has thirteen members, although some groups may choose to include more or fewer. Keeping the group small enables intimacy to grow among members and reduces the likelihood of developing into a pack of disciples led by a guru.

Why Thirteen Members?

Traditional covens have thirteen members. Why? A year contains thirteen lunar months. Wicca and Witchcraft are closely aligned with the moon and its feminine energy; thus, the number thirteen represents the lunar calendar and signifies wholeness.

Wicca and Witchcraft tend to appeal to people who dislike hierarchy and rigid dogma. Many modern Witches were raised in patriarchal religions that didn't encourage free thinking; they have chosen Wicca (or another pagan path) because it allows them to follow their own truth.

Covens offer a lot to practitioners of Wicca and Witchcraft. It's nice to have "kinfolk" with whom to share information about magick and spirituality. Covens provide an opportunity for learning on all levels. It's also fun to celebrate meaningful holidays and events with people who feel as you do. In a world that still doesn't completely accept Witches and magick, a coven brings individuals into a community where they can feel safe, accepted, and valued. Furthermore, the power a group can raise when they work together for the good of all far exceeds what one Witch could muster alone.

Benefits of Working with a Coven

You can learn a lot—about magick and life—through working with a coven. In particular, you will have the opportunity to:

- Learn what modern magick is in practice versus popular ideas and misrepresentations.
- Discover the history of a specific magickal tradition.

- Receive instruction on how to meditate and focus effectively (in a group setting).
- Learn how to raise and direct energy through group spells and rituals.
- Explore divine images and their meanings to a specific group.
- Acquire the tools of Witchcraft and use them in a coven setting.

Unless the group is eclectic, these points will be conveyed according to the coven's particular traditions, but that doesn't reduce the value of learning at the feet of good teachers. Everything you glean can (and will) be applied to other magickal methods and situations, either as a solitary Witch or within a group.

Coven Culture

The best covens are made up of individuals who take their responsibility to the group seriously. You want a group whose practices honor both the person and the Circle. Dedication, commitment, and work on the part of each individual are necessary to bring about a coven's strength and harmony. Consider the coven's tradition and the constructs that different traditions provide. Some covens follow specific "lineages" and ideologies, such as Celtic or Egyptian, Dianic or Alexandrian. If a coven holds to a particular tradition that doesn't interest you or with which you feel uncomfortable, you're in the wrong place.

Finding a Coven That's Right for You

How do you go about finding a coven to join? If you don't already know of a group, you could connect with one of the many online covens and pagan groups on the Web. Or, check bulletin boards at bookstores, health food cooperatives, yoga centers, and New Age shops. A nearby Unity or Unitarian Universalist Church could steer you in the right direction—it might even provide space for Circles and other spiritual events.

Use the Internet!

Modern Witches—and Witches-to-be—have a tremendous advantage over seekers twenty years ago. Today you'll discover a wealth of resources and information online. The first place to look is www.witchvox.com. Witchvox.com is the largest repository of information about the Craft, including listings of groups around the world.

As you decide whether a coven is right for you, ask yourself the following questions:

1. What kind of attendance and study requirements are expected of you?
2. Do these mesh with your schedules and responsibilities?
3. Does the group you're considering have a specific initiation ritual? What is it like? Is there anything in that ritual that doesn't fit your vision?
4. Does the group require secrecy? If so, what's the reason behind it and how hush-hush is everything?

Ask the coven leader for permission to attend an open Circle or other function before you consider pursuing membership. This will allow you to observe how the coven operates and how the people involved interact. Keep your senses open, allowing yourself to imagine what it would be like to work within that structure.

Only you can determine whether joining a coven is right for you, and if it is, which coven best suits your objectives. Take your time and don't rush. Bear in mind that every group you review will have its strengths, weaknesses, and idiosyncrasies—that is part of being human. Find a group with whom you feel a common bond and focus on the big picture; the nitpicky stuff you can work on over time.

Leadership and Members

If you're lucky, you'll find several groups to choose from. Pay particular attention to two key points: the aptitude of the leaders and the cohesiveness of the membership. These two factors can make or break a coven.

The best leaders don't seem to need titles. They are great facilitators, communicators, and honorable diplomats. They remain sensitive to the individuals and to the greater whole. They work hard to teach, inspire, and motivate the coven. When deciding between covens, ask yourself whether any of the leaders stand out as having these qualities and whether they have earned the respect of the coven for their wisdom, responsibility, openness, and consistency.

The best members are those who work together for the greater good, placing their individual preferences and desires second to the group's. They are dedicated to the group's goals and the magickal tradition to which they belong. They support and encourage one another, and refrain from gossiping, criticizing, or bickering among themselves. They welcome you into the collective and respect you, without judging or trying to control you. They willingly share information with you and seek your input.

Cautions and Caveats

If you see any of the following warning signs, the coven is probably not the best one to join.

1. Any group that says you must do something in a particular way, even if it goes against your personal taboos or moral guidelines, is not an ethical group.
2. Seeing members grovel before the coven's leader should raise a warning flag. A leader needs help and assistance, but should not order coven members around like servants.
3. Be wary of any coven that charges dues for membership, unless there is a valid reason for such fees (and proper accounting is in place). Most Witches believe that learning should be free. It's okay to ask for help with the gas, or munchies for a meeting, but there's a huge difference between this and making a fast buck off someone's spiritual thirst.

4. A group whose members brag about their numbers, claim they are all-powerful, or purport a 100 percent success rate in their magick isn't worth your time. There is no such thing as fundamental Wicca and no "right" way to pursue spiritual growth.

Initiation into a Coven

If you have found your ideal coven and would like to join, the next step is to ask the leader if the coven is open to new members and how to go about getting more involved. Find out when they hold initiations. The initiation is a very important moment of bonding. At this stage, coven members extend their Circle, in all its quirky intimacy, to another person. Every person in the group should be present for this activity. Each coven will enact its own, unique initiation ritual, even though there may be similarities from group to group. The ritual reflects the philosophy, traditions, objectives, and orientation of the group.

Welcoming Ritual

One nice welcoming ritual involves braiding or knotting yarn to symbolize that the new member's path is tied in with the rest of the coven. The initiate brings a length of yarn, which is tied into the bundle created by the current members. In some cases, the coven's priest or priestess will keep the bundle or wear it as a belt as a sign of office.

At the time of initiation, new members can choose the magickal names they wish to use in sacred space. They then go to each person present, introduce themselves by that name, and greet them as a brother or sister in the Craft (perhaps with a kiss on the cheek or a hug).

Forming Your Own Coven

Sometimes you can't find an existing coven that meets your needs. Or you may have belonged to a coven, but over time things have changed and it's time to try something else. If you don't wish to be solitary, you might consider forming your own coven.

Organizing a coven is kind of like baking. You need the right ingredients and timing to make everything turn out well. This isn't a social club, it's a spiritually mindful group and establishing it should be done with sincerity. Sometimes people form covens for the wrong reasons (for instance, to show off to friends or weird out the parents). Do some preliminary soul-searching—you really need to know yourself and be honest about your intentions.

Getting Down to Details

If you have determined this is the right move for you, decide how many people you want to be involved. Thirteen is the traditional number of Witches in a coven, but you don't have to follow that custom. Set a reasonable limit on membership. Quantity is less important than quality—in fact, a large quantity may diminish quality.

Next, ask yourself what kind of coven you want. Do you intend to focus on a specific magickal tradition? Do you want your group to be religious or secular? Do you want a rotating leadership or one defined leader? How will you choose the leader(s)? In other words, consider all the factors that will define and flesh out your group. These parameters will make it easier for others to decide whether your coven is right for them.

Here are some other issues to consider:

- What will the correct line of authority be?
- Will your coven work with magick for magick's sake, or will you be integrating religious aspects into your Craft?
- Where will your coven meet?
- Will you have requirements about how many meetings a year a person must attend to remain a member?
- Will you have study requirements?
- Will your members participate in activities together outside the coven setting?
- Do you plan to keep a Book of Shadows for your group (and if so, how and where will it be maintained)?

- Will you need to have specific tools or regalia for your coven meetings?
- What seasonal festivals will you observe?
- What other types of gatherings do you want to make available to your members (for instance, to respond to a member's personal needs)?
- What types of members' personal problems should the coven avoid getting involved in?
- How will someone attain the role of priest or priestess in your group?
- Who will make the decisions? Will you run your coven democratically, or will the leader's word be the final authority in every matter?

After these details have been ironed out, politely approach those individuals you think would be interested. Talk over the type of coven you envision and listen carefully to the way each person responds. It's okay for them to ask questions. If they don't, you should be worried. Nonetheless, somewhere at the bottom line, their vision of the group has to mesh with yours, or there are going to be problems.

Moving Forward

Once you've found a core group, the next stage is sort of a "waiting" period. Consider instituting a time period (for example, a year and a day) before anyone is considered a full, formal member of the coven (and before he or she is initiated into that group). This trial period gives everyone a chance to see if the relationship between the members is going to work. It also allows time to learn the skills necessary for working magick together. Rome wasn't built in a day, and neither is a good coven!

During this growing stage, try out a variety of rituals, spells, and meditations together, taking notes about each event. Find out what sensual cues work best for everyone. Note what goes really wrong, and what goes really right. By reviewing these notes regularly, you will begin to see the spiritual pattern you effectively use to build energy as a cohesive group.

At the end of the trial period, everyone should sit down and pow-wow. Discuss your accomplishments. Talk about what has and has not worked. Ask each person if he or she would like to continue in a more formalized manner. If the answer is yes, great! If not, separate as friends and spiritual helpmates. Just because you're not working magick together doesn't mean your other interactions will end.

Those who decide to move forward now have an even greater task ahead, that of keeping things going. Establish a line of authority and really start organizing. And, of course, it's time to start formally meeting as a coven.

Solitary Practice

Some Witches practice alone—in solitary—rather than with a group. Perhaps no coven is available, or a Witch may prefer to follow solitary practice because it suits her particular purposes, temperament, or lifestyle. Some people may work alone for a period, then join a coven for a period. Witches who don't belong to a coven may still gather with "kindred spirits" to celebrate the sabbats or other events, in a sort of extended Circle.

For seasoned Witches, a solitary path may be simply a choice. For the beginner, however, working alone can be lonely. It can also be more difficult than being guided by other, more experienced colleagues. On the other hand, a solitary pursuit enables you to develop your own style of magickal expression, rather than taking on the ideology or outward form of an established group. Fortunately, today many books—including this one—exist to teach a novice the basics of Wicca and Witchcraft.

As a solitary Witch—especially if you're just starting out—some guidelines can help you proceed safely and successfully:

- Read lots of books by different authors, to gain a variety of insights and perspectives.
- Meditate regularly to improve your mental focus and your connection with your higher self.
- Set a schedule for yourself that makes magickal study and work part of your everyday life.
- Apply what you learn—study alone won't make you a Witch.
- Start with simple rituals and spells, then work up to more complicated ones.
- Don't get discouraged if something doesn't work out the way you'd planned; try to determine what went wrong and why, and learn from your mistakes.
- Practice, practice, practice—magick is like every other skill: The more you do it, the better you get.
- Keep a journal (Book of Shadows) of your experiences.

After you've spent time studying and practicing on your own, you'll have a better idea of what type of magick appeals to you and which path you want to follow. At some point, you may decide to find a teacher or a group of like-minded individuals to work with. Working with a teacher can help you advance more quickly and may steer you away from some pitfalls along the way. Good teachers tend to be selective about the students they take on. If you can show that you've done your homework through solitary study, you'll have a better chance of convincing a teacher to help you reach the next level. Remember the old saying, "When the student is ready, the teacher will appear."

Creating Your Own Spells

It's fun to design your own unique spells. Personalizing spells makes them more meaningful. You can tailor any spell for specific purposes. If you're doing a love spell that calls for pink candles, but you want to turn up the heat, choose red candles instead. If you don't like the scent of lavender, you could use vanilla to dress a candle for a relaxation ritual.

And if you can't find a certain ingredient, it's okay to substitute another. For instance, ash leaves and basil both contain energies that can be used in protection spells. Blending ingredients allows you to fine-tune your magick to produce exactly the result you desire.

Another Use for Essential Oils

Essential oils can be added to water and misted into a room to work their magic. Or you can put a few drops in bathwater. You can also dress candles with them or heat them in an oil diffuser. The objective is to enliven your senses and stimulate your brain's limbic system, in whatever way pleases you.

Become familiar with various botanicals and stones, so you know which ones will serve your purposes best. Chapter 4 includes lists of herbs, oils, gemstones, and other ingredients to choose from when you're concocting your own spells. Learn which colors, numbers, and other symbols correspond to which intentions. Chapter 4 also provides information about symbolic connections.

Setting Up Shop

You don't need to purchase a warehouse full of supplies in the beginning. Start with a few basics: candles, incense, ribbons, and kitchen herbs. As you progress, add some quartz crystals and gemstones. Later on, you may wish to invest in a wand, chalice, athame, and pentagram. Tarot cards, a crystal ball, and a pendulum might follow at some point. Allow yourself to be led by your intuition. Build your collection as your need or interest dictates.

Sometimes magick items find you. People may give you tarot decks. You might find crystals lying on the side of the road. In time, you might decide to set up an extensive apothecary or grow your own magickal herbs. If not, accept the gifts that come find you anyway. Doing so demonstrates your openness to receiving the universe's bounty and keeps the circle of abundance operating smoothly. If, for some reason, a particular gift doesn't seem right for you, pass it on to someone else, but don't reject it.

Some Witches like to fashion their own candles or even distill their own scents. Others fabricate special ritual clothing or jewelry. Apply your talents however the muse guides you.

Use Your Imagination

When designing rituals and concocting spells, be creative. Use your imagination. The more involved you get in the process, the better. If you want to play a certain kind of music, by all means do so. If donning special garb helps you get into the mood, wear it. If you feel like dancing, singing, chanting, or experimenting with other movements, give it a try. Notice what you experience and record your impressions in your Book of Shadows.

It's fine to follow guidelines—and it's recommended in the beginning—but listen to your intuition, too. Don't be afraid to tweak a spell or vary a particular practice. After a while, you'll learn to connect with the energies of plants, stones, and other substances, and you can incorporate them harmoniously into your spells. Use your knowledge of the elements, correspondences, and symbols to come up with original spells.

Basic Spellworking Tips

As you go about designing your own spells and rituals, keep these basic guidelines in mind:

- Know what you want and state your intention simply, in the form of an affirmation.
- Refer to lists of ingredients—such as herbs, flowers, stones, oils, and colors—until you memorize them.
- Pay attention to the day of the week, moon phases, and other astrological factors.
- If you cast a Circle, abide by the rules of the ritual.
- If you're working with other people, be sure your intentions are in agreement.
- As the old adage goes, be careful what you ask for, because you just might get it.

Beyond these fundamentals, you're pretty much free to put your own personal spin on spells. Like a musician interpreting a composer's song, your unique rendition is as valid as anyone else's and may serve your purposes better than following a prescribed formula to the letter.

Living a Magickal Life

The Witch's world is rich and rewarding. Now that Witchcraft has "come out of the broom closet" and people around the world are sharing their knowledge openly, the field is growing ever richer. Everyone's experiences contribute to the development of the whole. Wicca and Witchcraft are not static ideologies; they are constantly evolving, just like the women and men who are part of these wisdom traditions.

Once you put on the Witch's mantle, your entire perspective will change. You'll never again see the world as you did before. You realize that nothing happens in a vacuum and nothing happens accidentally. You become aware of your connection with all life on Earth and with the universe, the physical and the nonphysical. You know that your thoughts create your reality, and everything you think, feel, and do affects the whole.

Being a Witch means living consciously, in harmony with the rest of existence to the best of your ability. It also involves using your will responsibly to produce the results you desire for yourself and others. According to Aleister Crowley, "Every intentional act is a magical act." As you move through the world as a Witch, you'll notice that everyone you meet is your teacher, and you in turn teach something to everyone you meet. Magick transforms you. Magick exists everywhere, all the time. You are part of the magick.

Index